Undercover Sex Signals

Undercover Sex Signals

Leil Lowndes

CITADEL PRESS
Kensington Publishing
www.kensingtonbooks.com

CITADEL PRESS BOOKS are published by

Kensington Publishing Corp.
850 Third Avenue
New York, NY 10022

First published by Agora Books, Baltimore. This edition has been entirely reset.

All Kensington titles, imprints, and distributed lines are available at special quantity discounts for bulk purchases for sales promotions, premiums, fund-raising, educational, or institutional use. Special book excerpts or customized printings can also be created to fit specific needs. For details, write or phone the office of the Kensington special sales manager: Kensington Publishing Corp., 850 Third Avenue, New York, NY 10022, attn: Special Sales Department; phone 1-800-221-2647.

CITADEL PRESS and the Citadel logo are Reg. U.S. Pat. & TM Off.

First Citadel printing: November 2006

10   9   8   7

Printed in the United States of America

Library of Congress Control Number: 2006929666

ISBN 0-8065-2793-5

Dedicated to the 96.7 percent of men in the world who don't pick up on a woman's obvious (to her!) sex signals. Here's help so you'll score with every pass you make.

Special thanks to O'Neals Bar & Grill in SoHo, New York City.

Contents

Section VI: Meeting to Mating (How to Win the Dating Game)

Undercover Sex Signals

You'll Never Have to Face Rejection Again

Meet Sandy, Ashley, and Jade, three of my four girlfriends, who have agreed to show you the 26 basic undercover sex signals. Why are they generously giving their time to do this? "Well," says Ashley, "we're tired of being hit on by men we don't want to talk to. But more than that, we're devastated that we're always throwing out signals to guys we do want to meet and they just don't get it! If this helps them know when to try and when not to, I'm all for it."

Jade said, "Sometimes it's very subtle. But we always let a gentleman know, through our body language, whether we'd like to make his acquaintance or not."

Sandy added, "You're damn right!"

1

Why Learn "U.S.S.s"?

Are you a relative rookie in the relationship game who stutters when talking to anyone wearing a skirt? Or are you a bit older with the personality, experience, polish, money, prestige, and charm to attract women? Either way, one thing is sure. Unless you are the rare man who picks up on a woman's subliminal sex signals, you are missing out on a lot of opportunities. Don't think the beauty at the end of the bar is going to beckon you by crooking her finger and winking at you. She casts far more subtle signals that 30 out of every 31 men miss.[1] They're called *undercover sex signals* or *U.S.S.s* and, if you don't bite immediately, she fishes for smarter tuna.

Going beyond sex for a moment (don't hyperventilate; I'll come back to it), let's talk about relationships. What are your chances of having a great one with a woman who, half the time, you have no idea how she's feeling or what she's hinting at? Or have you ever had a woman get all pissy and pouty on you—and you couldn't figure why? Watch out! That's as dangerous as lightning striking your zipper. It means you haven't been reading her (what she calls "obvious," and what you call "why the heck didn't she tell me?") signals. And unless you sharpen your sensitivity, she'll lay some high-heel tracks in the direction of "Outta here."

Gentlemen, what's the best compliment a woman ever gave you? Did she tell you you were brilliant? Witty? Handsome? Or was it a breathless, post-orgasmic "You're the best!" (I promised you I'd come back to sex.) My favorite compliment, bar none, was the time a man said, "Leil, you think like a man." For instance, I don't cotton to all that illusory romantic get-in-touch-with-your-inner-tadpole stuff. I don't like Ph.D.s or authors (although I am both) who pretend to have all the answers. Whenever I read advice on sex, I ask, "Says who?" Unless I see annotated studies in the back of a book proving what the writer says, I'm as suspicious as my geometry teacher when our whole back row got A+ on the final. So, like you, if I read an advertisement promising that "without saying a word, she's telling you she wants to meet you by giving off undercover sex signals," I want to know (1) what woman? (2) what signals? (3) how many signals? and (4) what each one means.

Get your calculators out, gentlemen. That kind of information is precisely what this book is going to give you, plus a whole lot more. It will demystify women in men's terms. It is precise, specific, definite, and substantiated material about the sometimes not-so-gentle sex. In school, you learned the 26 letters of the alphabet, and once you got the hang of it, you could read anything in English. Likewise, *Undercover Sex Signals* has 26 signals, and once you learn the patterns, you'll soon be able to read a woman as easily as your third-grade textbook.

Do you remember when you were a just a little shaver at the dentist's office and, to keep you from creating a ruckus waiting to be dragged into the torture chamber, the nurse gave you those "What's wrong with this picture?" game books? I do. There'd always be a couple of drawings with flags blowing in opposite directions, or a car with three wheels. The captions challenged our puny powers of perception by asking, "How many things can you find wrong in this picture?" Well, we're going to play an adult "X"-rated version of that game. Several of my girlfriends have agreed to show you

UNDERCOVER SEX SIGNAL #1:

The Girlfriend Gab

Seeing two women whispering about you like this can make a guy feel like they're saying, "Look at that jerk, the genetic mistake who just walked through the door. He'd have to soak *his jeans* in catnip to get a pussy cat to come near him." Wrong. Wrong. Wrong. Two women whispering about you is one of the oldest sex signals known to womankind. From the deepest jungles in Africa to the most sophisticated salons in Europe, girls will buzz when they spot a boy they like. Younger girls like Tanya on the left and Sandy on the right will probably giggle and or cuddle with each other while pointing you out.

Older, more sophisticated women will most likely try to hide the fact that
you are the subject of their discussion. But Ashley on the left and Jade on
the right are definitely open to your approach. How can you be sure? It's
because, in addition to whispering about you they are giving you two of
the classic undercover sex signals, which we'll discuss in a moment. Can
you guess what they are?

some of the moves they make when they spot a man they'd like to have more than "G"-rated communication with. And you're going to discover what's *right* with the picture—in other words, which girls are going to welcome your approach as well as which ones are going to treat you as if your mother didn't have any children. Look first at each picture and try to determine how she's feeling about you just from her body language. Then, and only then, read the caption.

For example, let's say you enter a club. In a booth on your left, you spot two young girls giggling and pointing at you. On a couch to your right, two older, more sophisticated women are whisperingly sizing you up. What do you suspect they're saying?

In case you didn't know it, chicks are forever sharing sexual secrets. Unfortunately however, many men become paranoid whenever they see two women looking at them and whispering. They fear the worst, and the last thing they think of doing is approaching the giggling twosome. This is a big mistake. The fact that two women are looking at you and whispering with each other means they definitely like you. It's too bad that women don't realize that two giggling girls could curdle the liver of even the most courageous guy. Fortunately, women usually outgrow the giggling part—but they still whisper when they spot a male they like.

2

How to Be a Sexual Sleuth

Let's analyze some of the U.S.S.s in the previous two photos. In the first, Tanya and Sandy in the booth are reacting like teens or even younger girls do when spotting a "really cute guy." Often, they will huddle together and touch each other while whispering—for two reasons. Not only does the touch feel good, but they're beginning to understand that most men enjoy seeing two women petting each other.

As women become more sophisticated, they will still whisper when spotting an attractive man just as Jade and Ashley are doing. But rather than giggling and petting each other, a little of the tiger in their tanks becomes active and they begin to compete for your attentions. Jade, on the right, is emulating a classic pinup, while Ashley, on the left, is trying to lure you over with a seductive smile.

Wait, there's more. Ashley is playing with her jewelry. This is an unmistakable sign of nervousness, or excess sexual energy. It doesn't take a Freudian analyst to figure out the symbolism of a woman stroking an object while maintaining eye contact with a man. Here's an extra hint: Be on special alert for which finger or fingers she uses to toy with her jewelry. A woman's middle finger is her most sensual one, and her ring finger comes in a close second. As this picture was being taken, Ashley was toying with her pearls between her middle finger and her ring finger, alternately wrapping them around each.

Unless you were sensitive to a woman's undercover sex signals, you might not think Jade is turned on to you; after all she is not smiling. What she's giving you, in fact, is a "triple whammy." Notice her 100 percent erect posture, which she snapped into when she saw you to give her torso more shape. And you can bet she's quite conscious of the fact that she is making her hair look more attractive by primping. When you become a real U.S.S. man, you'll also notice she is not fluffing her hair with her knuckles toward you but with her palm in front. This, in conjunction with her other signals, is as good as an engraved invitation for you to come talk to them.

Look for "Clusters" of Sex Signals

Now the bad news. The millisecond women spot you, their brains go into overdrive. You are on trial. The way you move, the way you acknowledge them, and the way you deal with everyone else in the room becomes cold hard data that they briskly program into their callous mental computers. (Well, at least you don't need to wait long for your report card. They show it to you almost instantaneously.)

Everyone has a different level of expertise in reading people. On a scale of 1 to 10, a female's expertise averages an 8 or 9. A male's usually hovers around a 2. I may be preaching to the choir here, because perhaps you're the rare man (one in 31) who can read a woman's signals. Unfortunately, most guys are like mosquitoes in a nudist colony when they see women they want. They know what to do, but they don't know where to start. For that reason only, I'm going to begin with *very* basic material that may seem obvious to you. Then we'll progressively get more advanced until you've mastered the entire alphabet of 26 female moves. No more mystery. No more insecurity about making the move. No more, "I wonder if she's going to welcome my approach or blow me off."

You will soon know why women play such circuitous games when it comes to sex and dating. We'll talk about undercover signals—whether they're learned or instinctive—and even about how to exude a few of your own. Near the end of the book, when you're an expert in reading women, you'll be able to spot sex signals as clear as rabbit pills in a sugar bowl, and you'll know precisely what to do in response to each. Imagine being able to walk into a party and being able to say, "Ah ha! The blonde by the bar is giving me the No. 20 and the redhead over there is casting me the old U.S.S. 13."

When a woman slings out the ole 13, she assumes you know she is definitely interested. The sad truth is that nobody ever told you that if, while maintaining eye contact, she pulls her hair aside to bare her neck, it is U.S.S. No. 13 called *The Necking*, an instinctive "I submit" signal. (Even dogs know that.) And you just thought she was feeling the heat.

But not to worry. As you close the last page of this book and stash it at the bottom of your closet so well a psychic couldn't find it (highly recommended since your crystal ball predicts a plethora of female visitors in your very near future), you'll be able to read a roomful of women faster than Evelyn Wood can read a stop sign.

Wait, gentlemen, there's more. You will find priceless little insights into the multilevel madness of the female brain scattered throughout the text in little boxes called "Chick-lets." Think of them as road signs for navigating your way around the all-female planet of Venus. When you've chewed on these "Chick-lets" for a while, you could be a certified Venetian tour guide

Now, lest you think I'm overstating the case, *Undercover Sex Signals* is not going to turn every 97-pound weakling into a Mr.

Universe with women overnight. But it does assure that you'll never get verbal sand kicked in your face again by any woman you approach.

Nor will you find any lofty prose between the covers of this manual. I'm not even going to submit it for the Pulitzer Prize. Awright, so the whole thing checks in at about an 8th-grade reading level. But, gospel truth? Yes. Everything in *Undercover Sex Signals* is based on nonbiased sociological, biological, anthropological, and psychological studies—as well as personal observations and a consensus of what beautiful women have confided to me over the years. If you read something about women and the information I provide is not sufficient proof, then I beseech you to check the referenced numbers in the notes. There you will find the original studies cited.

Be forewarned, however, that most of them are written in a strange dialect called "Academeeze," with an average reading time of 10 minutes per sentence. I translated them into plain English (too plain for some people's taste).

But, whether you decide to dig down to the original source or are satisfied with the soft-x simplified translation, you can be assured that everything you read is substantiated, authenticated, and certified. The most skeptical hairsplitting nitpicker won't find a nit of fiction to pick in this treasure trove of truth.

It's Not K.I.S.S.

This book is not one of those K.I.S.S. (keep it simple, stupid) books on body language that say that each movement has an irrefutable meaning by itself. Men, especially, have to be wary of being too logical and assuming that each gesture by itself incontrovertibly reveals a specific emotion. Reading her undercover sex signals can be likened to reading letters of the alphabet. The letters seldom have meaning by themselves, but they form words when linked together. The signals by themselves are not a true indication of her emotions. But linked together, in what are called "gesture clusters," they are extremely revealing. In fact, a woman's words can lie. But it takes one well schooled in the art of deceit to lie with her body.

Just like letters of the alphabet seldom mean much when standing alone, the 26 sex signals we're going to learn are not conclusive by themselves. The mere fact that a woman caresses her arm while looking at you or dangles a shoe while talking with you does not mean she's suddenly struck with an irresistible desire to roll over and say, "Do me." It could just mean that her arm itches or her feet hurt. If, however she does both and then flips her hair or licks her lips, you can start to get the picture. Just as kids learn the alphabet before they can write out "Dick and Jane have a dog named Spot," it's advisable to learn all 26 signals before you start thinking about Dick doing Jane on the spot.

We discussed the cluster of signals going on in photos 2 and 3. In the rest, we'll concentrate on the primary sex signal but also be on the lookout for the secondary ones. There will be a quiz at the end. (Hey, I warned you this was going to be 8th-grade.)

3

It's Tough Being
a Guy Today

It's tough being a guy today, especially when it comes to relationships. Granted, you guys have us beat at kicking a football, pinning a guy to the mat, squeezing a beer can, and, when you're feeling real good, even ripping an occasional phone book in half. But, as I'm sure you'll be the first to admit, you are punch-drunk after the first round of that rough-and-tumble, give-and-take combat sport called "relationships."

Take an average night at an average bar for an average guy. One minute, he'll swear that not-so-average redhead in the corner is giving him a seductive Julia Roberts smile and a "C'mon over here, Big Boy" look that would make Larry Flynt blush. An hour later, he's staring into his refrigerator speculating on the safety of the 3-week-old Chinese leftovers and wondering why she cut him off when he took her up on her *obvious* invitation.

While he nukes the nibbles, his mind wanders back to a conversation he had last week with his best buddy's girlfriend, Lisa. She's telling him how disappointed her girlfriend Alexis, that voluptuous blonde visitor from California was, when he "didn't pick up on her *obvious* come-on signals."

"Her whaaat?" he asked Lisa. "The only thing obvious about her was . . ." He'd wisely decided against finishing the sentence and faked a credible cough.

Now he's noodling on what Lisa and Ms. L.A. could have thought was so *obvious* that he missed. "I'm a meathead," he mutters to himself while scraping mildewed moo goo gai pan into the garbage.

Before you start getting too hard on yourselves, fellas, realize that females have a head start on you on picking up and sending out subtle sex signals—by at least a decade. It's like sports. Any athlete, or wannabe athlete, knows how important a 10-year head start is. A kid who didn't pass a pigskin until he was 17 wouldn't have a prayer of becoming a pro. But little girls started on the relationship game back in the sandbox.

While you and the guy-kid who lived next door were early male bonding by tying your cats' tails together, your pre-teen sisters were female bonding by discussing kids of the male gender in painstaking detail. They analyzed every word a guy said. And what he *really* meant when he said, "Pass the mashed potatoes, please." They examined every syllable, every expression, and every gesture for every nuance of meaning. When they finished, they reexamined it again in case they missed something the first time around. It comes naturally for women. It's in their genes.

She's Tuned, 24 Hours a Day, to a Station You Can't Even Hear

I'm not kidding. Neurosurgeons can point to clumps of neurons in female brains that cause women to stay tuned 24 hours a day to the same station, WYAT (What You Are Thinking). Even through heavy static, they understand every word. They even hear it when you're silent and you think you're off the air. They discuss with one another your thoughts and feelings, ones that you didn't even know you had!

Conversely, guys do *not* exactly ponder a woman's psychology—or their own for that matter. You, of course, are rational. That means if you're like most guys, you have a guy brain, which is an analytical, problem-solving type organ. You don't like things to be nebulous and vague like all those fuzzy relationship things. You prefer to define people in measurable terms (like his batting average or her breast size).

Lawyers are no ninnies. They knew about all that Mars and Venus stuff long before John Gray decided to get cute with his different planets. The venerable barristers may battle for equal pay and equal work (if they're paid enough or the heat is on); when it comes to their own turf, however, they do an about-face on job discrimination. In their textbook for attorneys on choosing jurors (voir dire), two law professors stress the importance of having an assistant on hand—female, of course—solely for the purpose of watching the prospective juror's body language.[2]

Why female? Because if the courtroom lawyer is defending, say, a police officer against alleged police brutality, he or she doesn't want a closet cop-hating grenade with a short fuse sitting in the jury box. So naturally the legal eagle needs a better bird dog to pick up distant early warning signals about the dude's rage.

The three most crucial qualifications for the job of picking up on body language and other hidden signals?

The first qualification: Being female.

The second qualification: Being female.

The third qualification: Being female.

In other words, males need not apply.

4

Proof That Women
Are Bird-Dogging You
(and You Don't Know It)

Unless you're suffering from bad breath, bad posture, and a really bad attitude, women are chasing you. Well, to be absolutely accurate, perhaps the woman *you* want is not hot on your tail. But, by sheer law of averages, unless you're a mental or physical disaster, three or four women in every situation you find yourself in probably have their eyes on you. At a party or a bar, a woman notices *every* man who walks in the door. If she doesn't write him off immediately, she throws out obvious "come meet me" signals. But the friendly owner of the Chinese restaurant down my block tells me he sells "rots of food to single male customers very rate at night." What does that mean? It means that men are missing women's signals, a shameful situation that we are going to remedy right now.

People often ask me why women are more adept than men at reading subliminal signals. Again, Mother Nature downloaded 90 percent of the nurturing instincts into the female of our species. Suppose a mother didn't know how to read body language. A hungry baby with a full diaper would have to wait a long time for a square meal and a change if its mother had to depend on the spoken word.

This talent also comes in handy when *she* wants something. In previous economic societies, little boys were trained to go out and capture what they wanted—whether that meant bringing home a bear for dinner or, more recently, a sales contract to pay for dinners. Little girls are trained, even now, to use their wiles to get what they want. "Oh, Daddykins, I'd just love a brand-new bicycle." And, of course, catching "Daddykins" in the right mood is crucial to her successful acquisition.

As little girls get older, however, the stakes get higher, and their skill becomes more fine-tuned. Now the little girl who wanted that bicycle is all grown up, she wants a mink coat, and "Daddykins" is no longer related by blood. "Sugar Daddykins" and all the other men in her life are astounded by her ability to interpret little signals.

The Biggest Difference Is Not Your Plumbing

I'm sure you've noticed by now that women have breasts and you don't. (If not, this book is too advanced for you. Get your money back and buy some glasses.) Women also excel at the spoken language—like making you feel like a worm when you forget their birthdays or when you can't verbalize one good excuse for stumbling in at 3 a.m. And, unfortunately, women know their way around better when it comes to the subtleties of a relationship. You can't understand why your girlfriend accuses you of being an insensitive clod at the party when you and your long-lost college compadre, your amigo, your good old buddy-roo, went into a second hour of old college-football stories.

Don't blame women; they can't help it. It's all in their minds—literally. Neurologists have utilized new technologies like functional magnetic resonance imaging (FMRI) and positron emission tomography (PET) to catch men's and women's brains right in the act. They track their respective gray matter when they're thinking, giving off or picking up signals, feeling, forgetting, or remembering. (You can explain *that* biological difference to her the next time you forget her birthday.)

So after many decades of pondering, presuming, and postulating on whether men and women really differ in anything but their privates, scientists have determined—hand me the envelope—YES! When teenage boys say to teenage girls, "Geez, you and I are on different wavelengths," they called it right. Final answer: Men and women think and communicate in dramatically different ways. Here is your first "Chick-let" to chew on:

Women even *interpret* things in vastly different ways than guys do. You can say something you think is nice to a woman and get an iced drink in your face. Or a woman you thought was crazy about you suddenly issues you walking papers. How are you supposed to know that you'd better put up your guard whenever she says, "You're a nice guy"—because that means the ax is coming soon?

> Realize that when it comes to verbal warfare, chicks have a distinct neurological advantage over you. If she wants to "discuss something," don't get caught off guard! Say anything to DELAY the argument so you'll have time to think. Oh, and use the word "sorry" when you ask for a delay. Chicks love it.

Quite rightly you protest, "if she wants to break up with me, why doesn't she just say she despises me, she can't stand to breathe the same air as I do, and she never wants me reflected in her eyeballs again?"

The answer is obvious, at least to the entire female population. She doesn't want to hurt your *feelings*. It clearly, starkly, and simply means that you haven't committed sufficient evil to merit a major lambasting and she feels guilty about telling you you're history. So, instead of saying that, she says, "You're a nice guy."

Then a week later, sure as a dead man sinks, comes her comment that "You're *too* nice for me." She lets another week pass, and then comes the final ax. It's the old guillotine-in-slow-motion scene, one of the oldest gambits known to womankind. She's genuinely convinced that ripping your heart to pieces shred by shred is kinder than saying "I find you utterly reptilian, and you make my skin crawl. Get lost!"

> Incidentally, don't make the same mistake. When it's time to break up, do it the guy way—with quick, clean tears. And above all, do not talk about her to your next girlfriend. No matter how much you diss your ex, your new lady will think you're still holding a torch for her. A chick wants to feel that your every brain cell, when you're together, is devoted to her.

Then, to top it off, women are becoming pickier than ever before in history. Gentlemen, if you look around you, you'll see you are surfing on a major societal tidal wave where the sexy, gutsy, single, and horny gal is the heroine on the big screen, the little screen, in fiction, and increasingly in *fact*. Coming soon to a place near you— in droves—women who see what they want and have the courage to go after it.

But here's the big difference. They're more apt to tire of you first, and then they will drop you with not so much as a "thank you very much." A recent CNN/TIME poll found that more women than men are refusing marriage or a long-term live-in relationship until the Perfect Partner comes along.[3]

Let me be perfectly clear on this. The 21st century seductress doesn't exactly spot you, point a long, red-acrylic-nail-tipped finger at you, and say, "Hey, you! Yes, you, Big Boy. I want you. Come with me." But she now has the courage to send out signals—dozens of signals—that are as clear as crystal to her, and as clear as mud to you.

Gentlemen, first the good news: If you play your cards right, you can both have a great time—and when it's over, it's over. Less trouble, fewer tears, fewer entanglements, and less "Why are you afraid to commit?" If you perfect your perceptions, you can see her for a while, have sex, say "Sayonara," and still be an ethical dude.

Now the bad news: You have to learn the language, a new language called *Undercover Sex Signals* (*U.S.S.* for short). You have to detect and decipher such signals, or you're going to be eating a lot of Chinese leftovers.

Gentlemen, a final word to the wise: You might be tempted to skip from photo to photo in this book, but that won't give you the whole story. You will be a bigger winner with a woman when you see her signals in their full sociological framework and learn how to react to each one. There is more to come in *U.S.S.* than just an analysis and an explanation of her signals. You will be given (almost) idiot-proof hints about how to become a virtuoso with women, a maestro if you will. I'll tell you what makes a champion in women's eyes and what makes a chump (and what a lot of champions did to become instant chumps and what a lot of guys chicks thought were chumps did to transmogrify themselves into champions).

Some unprincipled suitors think lying and cheating to steal a woman's heart and get her into bed is fair play. A Pyrrhic victory perhaps, but one that leaves you alone and having to mobilize again for the next conquest. (Apropos of principles, after this project is finished, I want to sleep well at night, not fearing I have given you unethical artillery to force your fair lady's surrender.) I'm assuming that your desire is to meet women with whom you might form meaningful relationships, not bodies to seduce, hurt, and then desert. It is in that spirit that I'll give you, under oath, "the truth, the whole truth, and nothing but the truth" as it has never been revealed before.

I will answer all the questions you've been dying to ask about women, questions like: "What turns women on, and what turns them off?" "Why are so many women attracted to bad boys?" "Are there any good opening lines?" "Why do women always travel to the restroom in packs of four?" . . . and so on. You get the picture.

At this point, you may be asking, "Why are you, who previously has been sworn to secrecy, revealing this now?" Well, for two reasons. The first is, as corny as it may sound, a sincere dedication to wanting to help people. *Undercover Sex Signals* will definitely help men in their pursuit of women—a pursuit we women desperately want you to be successful at.

The second reason is that my publisher offered me a very tidy sum to rat on my sisters. For the money I'm getting, I'd rat on my 86-year-old grandmother who has a nasty habit of swiping sugar packs from the local diner.

Enjoy the book and follow the advice. Soon, you'll be in the diary of every dame in town!

5

Only One Man in 31
Is Hep to Her Sex Signals

One of the most common complaints I hear from my girlfriends is "He must be gay. I mean, I was so obvious. Didn't he know I was trying to let him know I was interested?" Many of the women I've known and worked with were so beautiful and so confident that they just knew that if the guy was single and didn't respond, he was either blind, gay, madly in love with someone else, or worried about a jealous girlfriend who packs a pistol in her purse. What my friends refused to believe was that the men were only blind to their signals.

Decades of being an incurable people watcher and studying interpersonal relationships has made me a great fan of a Dr. Timothy Perper, who is one of the most respected researchers in male/female courting behavior.

His laboratory? A singles bar.

His subjects? Unsuspecting men and women who were there for the purpose of meeting each other.

With the resolve of a mad scientist examining horny hamsters, Dr. Perper spent 9,000 grueling hours sitting on a bar stool and feverishly taking notes on cocktail napkins while watching women and couples. Those beer-soaked scribbles became the research for getting his doctorate. (How cool is that?) Subsequently, Dr. Perper's work has become one of the most esteemed bodies of research on male/female interaction that the world has to date.

His conclusion: (Read this carefully, guys.)

> *Women have vested nearly all their actions with symbolic meaning. Physical distance, topic of conversation, degree and intensity of eye contact, and choice of locale have all been assigned an exquisitely developed and coordinated set of proceptive and rejective meanings. Women employ their total environment symbolically: everything and every act in it consciously expresses how they feel about the man.*[4]

Translation: "Women are constantly giving off undercover sex signals."

Dr. Perper continues,

> *We cannot conclude, however, that women actually succeed in communicating with men through these symbolic meanings. In part that depends on what he thinks the woman's behavior means. Profound chasms of misunderstanding can exist between men and women concerning these meanings . . . The skilled objective observer, therefore, has little trouble understanding the woman's intentions, even if her male partner can't.*[5]

Translation: "But guys just don't get it."

"Yo," you're probably thinking, "you mean there is rock-solid proof that babes are giving me the come-on and I'm as blind as a potato?" You called it. That's precisely what I mean. If you have the powers of observation of the average guy, you don't know a "C'mon" from "Get lost!"

Dr. Perper further proved this point by surveying his subjects as they left the bar, either singly or together. One of the questions buried in his survey was "Do you think the woman you were talking with (or are leaving with now) likes you?" Practically all of the men responded with a less than erudite, but very truthful, form of "Uh, gee, I dunno." 30 out of every 31 men had missed the signals the woman was emitting.[6]

6

Why Can't a Woman Communicate More Like a Man?

Henry Higgins in "My Fair Lady" called it when he said women were "exasperating, calculating, agitating, maddening, and infuriating." Don't be embarrassed if you don't understand the fairer sex. Practically since the beginning of time, male philosophers, psychologists, and just plain guys have been as stumped as woodpeckers in the Petrified Forest over what makes females tick.

One of the reasons men can't figure what makes a woman "tick" is that, when it comes to men, her head is "ticking" all the time. Forget about "just having fun." From the moment you open your mouth, you are being "auditioned" for a long-term romance. So, be careful! Don't make any first- date references to your own emotional baggage. Hers will be enough for you to carry!

Researchers have successfully studied the mating habits of female rabbits, hamsters, and fish and come to a consensus. No problem. But just when they thought they had the answer on the female of the human species, their theories went down the drain, because thousands of exceptions reared their pretty heads. Philosophers from Aristotle to Zoroaster scratched their ivory domes over the strange signals women give off when they are sexually attracted to someone. So did scientists from Archimedes to Vivtruvius, poets from Auden to Yeats, and religious leaders from Amish to Zen Buddhists. One of science's superstars, Sigmund Freud, made a big proclamation on love before he died. He declared,—are you ready—"Well, we know very little about love." (Now, there's a scientific observation if I ever heard one. But what do you expect from Freud? He didn't even know whether his cigar was just a cigar or a sex symbol.)

But questions about love were not going to be buried with Freud. Giving scientists an unanswered question is like giving an elephant a bag of peanuts. They began cracking open every shell of evidence they could find. Naturally, scientists started where they always start: with the obvious. They had no trouble analyzing human physical reactions when they felt tired, angry, thirsty, hungry, etc. But they were still totally flummoxed by "this thing called love."

In the middle of the 20th century, a generation of Americans opened their ears and their minds when superstar scientist, anthropologist, explorer, writer, and teacher Margaret Mead spoke. As head of the Department of Anthropology at the American Museum of Natural History, she often looked at other cultures to help her compatriots better understand the complexities of the human animal. So, naturally everyone assumed she was correct when, observing the cockamamie things men and women the world over do in the name of love, she told us that sex signals are all "learned." She said, "We may safely say that many, if not all, of the personality traits which we call 'masculine' and 'feminine' are as lightly linked to sex as are the clothing, the manners, and the form of headdress that a society at a given period assigns to sex."[7]

Peekaboo! (Not for Little Babes Only)

Unfortunately for Margaret Mead's theory, too many exceptions rose to the surface about her ideas. Obviously, no one carefully teaches a Tahitian girl to play peekaboo behind a bamboo leaf to lure a man across the tropical clearing. And as far as we know, no modern-day girls in North America had their mothers train them to play peekaboo over their menus with strange men in a restaurant. From childhood, they knew that concealing their face builds up the excitement of anticipation.

Unfortunately, many men misinterpret a woman's signals. If, for example, you walked into a room and saw a woman looking at you from behind the menu as Ashley is, would you assume she is thinking, "You, yes you, come talk to me—now" Or "Eek, let me hide behind this menu so you don't come hit on me."

Ashley is giving you a classic U.S.S. and is casting the opening salvo in the age-old peekaboo game. She learned it from her daddy when she was still in the crib. He'd hide his eyes behind closed fingers; the longer he stayed hidden, the bigger the babe's (when she was a *real* babe) glee would be when he peeked through them and said "peekaboo."

UNDERCOVER SEX SIGNAL #2:

The Peekaboo

Here Ashley has obviously spotted a man she'd like to have come talk to her. Women are especially fond of playing peekaboo, because they probably played it as babies with their fathers. Daddy would hide his eyes, and then, upon his revealing them, she would giggle and squeal with delight. The longer the eyes are concealed, the greater the tension and the more enticing it is when smiling mischievous eyes are revealed. Big girls throughout the ages have played peekaboo with their fans or masks at masked balls.

Now, gentlemen, upon being given this peekaboo invitation, should you make a beeline for her? Absolutely not. She has not summoned you yet. Approaching now would be premature. She has merely extended an obvious invitation to play the game with her. What would you do if Ashley were looking over her menu at you like this?

> Remember that chicks play the courting game entirely differently than men do. They love your stolen glances across a crowded room, the games of peekaboo, the slight tension, and your hints of adulation. And you have to learn to play the game the way the girls like it—if you want to play with the girls, that is.

If Ashley wants to start this nonverbal play, you will do far better if you slow down and match her at her own game for a while. As in love-making, she wants a little more foreplay to the meeting than you do. She has handed you the opportunity to make her feel like a southern belle, fluttering her feathered fan, raising and lowering it provocatively. If your foreplay to the meeting is good, she'll want to go through with it. If it isn't, she'll write you off.

> Your responding "guy sex signal" should always match the intensity and style of her signal. Take your cue from her, whether the lady you've just fallen in lust with is the preacher's daughter at the church social or a gal at a brothel whose tombstone will read, "The only time she ever slept alone."

How to Indulge in Step-by-Step "Foreplay" from Across the Room

Here's how to play Ashley's game. Since she's offered a tiny half-smile, you should do the same. Then, instead of approaching immediately, pick up a menu and pretend to be engrossed in it for a moment or two. Then, it's time to "notice" Ashley again. This time, tilt the menu forward to look at her. Keep your eyes on her until she starts to squirm a little and look down. (Don't worry, she's loving it.) If she likes you, she will look up again—at which point you should give a small smile and again, hide your face behind the menu.

Repeat this sequence a few times and watch her smiles gradually widen, opening the door for conversation. At this point, it is quite appropriate to tell the waiter you'd like to buy her a drink, but, instead of letting her know who ordered it, the waiter should just say, "An admirer wanted you to have this." She'll know who that admirer is!

Corny? You bet. Old-fashioned? You'd better believe it. But for the U.S.S. man, it works every time. Dr. Perper said it best: "If your foreplay to the meeting is good, she'll want to go through with it. If not, she'll write you off." Translation: *Learn to play her game, or lose the dame.*

7

Using U.S.S.s to Determine
If She's Interested

Suppose you spot a lady sitting across the room who's looking around acting like your mother didn't have any children who lived. You examine the situation and can't detect a trace of a U.S.S. coming from her. Is the game lost?

Absolutely not. Now is the time for you to skillfully cast some of your own U.S.S. bait to see if she bites. A smile is always good bait, but most men are as confused as goats on Astroturf when the woman doesn't smile back. They read that as "Rejection" with a capital "R" While licking their wounds, they wonder why some guys have the edge with women and they don't. It's doubly confusing to them because a lot of those guys getting all the action aren't even good-looking and some have dud personalities. Yet they never seem to get the old heave-ho. Women greet them enthusiastically. Why is that?

It's very simple. The successful man never gets rejected, because he tests the waters first. He then systematically follows the sequence of signals that Dr. Perper and I have repeatedly seen work with women. Some of it may seem contrived (it definitely is), but here is what has been *proven* to work best when trying to pick up a hottie.

Positioning is all important. Whether you are at a party, at a parade, or in a park, when you first see the woman you want to meet, jockey yourself into position so you are in her direct line of sight. Try to arrange it so she can see you head to toe. That way, she can check you out and when you do approach she will not find you intimidating.

Then keep a friendly and gentle gaze focused on her. Eventually, she will sense that you are looking at her and will look up. So far, so good. Then you give her a small respectful nod and a smile. She will look away. That's how she's been programmed. Expect it. *This does not mean she is not interested!* She is merely giving you the most common sex signal known to womankind, *The Shy Geisha*.

The Single Most Common U.S.S.— and Men Think It's Rejection!

It is at this point that non-U.S.S. savvy men mess up. When a man looks at a woman, she will almost always look away. Women in the most remote African jungle do it. Women in the sophisticated salons of Paris do it. Women at Friday's restaurant do it. Women all over the world do it. It's part of the courtship rite. In primitive societies, the less sophisticated ones even put their hands over their eyes or their mouths and giggle. Even in today's more modern Western civilization, however, the best you can expect is a barely detectable softening of the lips or a tiny suppressed smile as she looks away.

UNDERCOVER SEX SIGNAL #3:

The Shy Geisha

Ashley is looking away, feigning modesty. But be certain she is very open to your approach. Why? Because she is looking *down* and away. (If she were not interested, her eyes would stay on the same level or look up and away.) What should you do when she gives you those "shy-geisha" eyes? Keep looking in her direction; if she looks up again within 45 seconds, it confirms her interest in you.

Eye contact is where the rubber really hits the cement in sexual attraction. The way she looks at you reveals a woman's true emotions. The U.S.S. man who knows how to read a woman's eyes never needs to fear rejection.

When you smile at women who don't know you, practically every one of them will demurely (or strategically) look away. But the *way* the woman looks away tells all. If she looks down toward the floor and away, sweeping the floor as it were with her eyes, it means she likes you. That's the "shy-geisha" look we're talking about here. Dr. Perper proved that if she then looks up again within 45 seconds, she does indeed want and expect that you will make a move on her.

Do be aware that when you do approach her, she may not openly show her pleasure. Some women feel that you will be more attracted to them if they play "hard to get." But since she has given you the "geisha-eyes" signal you can be assured she is very pleased by your attentions.

Let's explore some other reactions she might have when you smile at her. Suppose she looks away horizontally on a flat plain, as though her eyes were dusting the walls. This indicates that she's not sure she wants to talk with you and her internal jury on you is still sequestered. Now it's advisable to wait, smile at her again, or make some other impressive move before you get the verdict on whether you will ever be guilty of stealing her attention from the other guys.

The third possibility is a bummer. If she looks toward the ceiling and away, it means that she is essentially rolling her eyes at you. She is probably not interested or is otherwise involved, maybe both. Forget it and move on to another chick.

Even if you have received either the first or second response, do not make the approach immediately. It is the time to give her a second smile. Most likely, she will respond to your second smile much as she did to the first.

For surefire answers to questions like "Does she like me?" and "Shall I make the move?" employ the old "eyeball test." And, remember, it's not a question of whether or not she looks away. It's *how* she looks away that counts—down, sideways, or up.

Now is the time to make the approach. You should walk toward her, in full view if possible, and stand close enough to talk, but not too close. The reason you want to be in full view is that you want her to see all of you so that she can feel more relaxed about talking with you. Approaching another man head-on could be considered aggressive. But it is the most strategic way to approach a female in a social setting. Keep a respectful distance, yet one that permits easy conversing. The precise distance will vary depending on the room size, the crowd, the situation, and certain other variables.

More Eyeways

There is a third signal you should keep your antenna tuned to. See if you can catch any women giving you quick, furtive sideways glances. Because society frowns on a woman making a too-obvious play for a man, a lot of women will just keep glancing over at you, primarily to see if you are noticing them. That, gentlemen, is a sure sign that a woman is interested and will be sorely disappointed if you don't make a move on her.

UNDERCOVER SEX SIGNAL #4:

The Sidelong Glance

Here Jade seems to be at peace, sitting at the bar preferring not to be interrupted. But the U.S.S. man knows the truth. She wants to be approached by the guy she's eyeballing out of the side of her eyes.

An Anthropologist Bites the Dust

Back to the history books for a moment. The time was right for
Margaret Mead's politically correct argument. After all, in the middle of the last century, Americans wanted to feel that men and
women were not so different from each other after all. (Of course,
that lie never fooled the French, who just shrug and say *Vive la difference!*) So the ancient battle of "nurture vs. nature" didn't score
the knockout Maggy Mead thought it would. Why? Because some
then-recent findings yanked her argument right out of the ring.
Women the world over were playing peekaboo with everything
from jungle leaves to silk fans; and since they were flirtatiously letting their kimonos, grass skirts, saris, sarongs, sundresses, and
denim blouses fall open at strategic moments to reveal strategic
body parts, Margaret Mead's "It's all learned" theory was down for
the count.

8

Little Girls and Little Guys Are Different from Blastoff

When kids were brought up in *identical* environments, researchers found female toddlers reacting in very different ways from their male counterparts. For example, in kindergarten, if one little girl was crying, the others would huddle around her and try to dry her tears, whereas little boys usually carried on with their little-guy pursuits, seemingly oblivious to the howling and bawling of one of their tiny compadres.[8]

Does that mean that little boys are callous? Of course not. Letting their buddy bawl is a "sign of respect" to little guys. Little girls think it's "neglect." This is just one example in hundreds of how males and females react differently from the get-go. Is it any wonder, then, that women signal their sexual interest to a stranger in a vastly different way than men do? And is it any wonder that guys just don't get it?

Even something as subtle as playing with her necklace or twisting an earring while looking at a man can speak volumes in the hidden language of female sex signals. And here's the rub: Women expect you to pick up on these hints.

"Why in the world would playing with her necklace mean 'I want sex' to her," you might rightly ask. Well, the action serves a

UNDERCOVER SEX SIGNAL #5:

The Jewelry Tug

In this picture, Jade is giving you what she thinks is a very clear invitation to make a move on her. She is looking right at you, and she assumes you know that by her direct eye contact, coupled with her playing with her necklace, you understand she means "C'mon over!" Happily, this signal gives you the perfect opener. You can smile at her, approach, and then compliment her jewelry.

dual purpose. First, it instinctively feels good to tug on an earring or twist a necklace between her fingers. Second, when a woman maintains eye contact with you while playing with her jewelry, she is drawing attention to her "decoration," her plumage if you will.

Are Sex Signals Rocket Science?

While they're not exactly rocket science, I can see how these signals can make a guy feel like a mouse in a maze. And to further complicate matters, women often use two or three at once. One of the 26 basic signals is usually more prominent than the others, but it is backed up by support signals. Although Jade is obviously using the *"jewelry fondle"* on you, for example, she is also playing a little bit of peekaboo with her hair over one eye.

A study published in the professional research journal *Sex Roles* proved how stiff men are when it comes to giving off, let alone picking up, subtle signals of affection, even friendly ones to their buddies.[9]

Think about your best buddy, the pal you'd stick with through thick and thin. You'd race to the ramparts with a broken beer bottle to defend him. In short, you love the guy. But you're a rare man indeed if you've ever done more than high-five him and say, "Hey, great to see ya, buddy." Another study found that if straight men wish to express their fondness for each other, they choose a public place, preferably an emotionally charged one like a wedding, a funeral, or a college-graduation ceremony, and then let it all hang out—for about three seconds. Then, according to the study, they often feel embarrassed and glance around to make sure no one was watching their fleeting bonding moment.[10]

Why is it so brief? The answer is obvious (to you that is). That's how you guys strengthen the bond and retain unquestionable stud status. But you both know how you feel about each other. And that's cool. Women wouldn't want you any other way.

But here's the point. If 95 percent of red-blooded American males have an unusual way of communicating feelings that women don't understand, is it any wonder that women have a way that men don't understand? Picking up a woman's "come hither" signals makes a guy feel like he's watching her in a house of mirrors that are all spinning at once.

One of the problems is that guys are too logical. For example, when a woman lets a shoe dangle on her toes, or loosens her clothing, your rational guy-brain figures she just has a nervous habit or it's getting warm. Not so. When a woman is in the presence of men, she is intensely aware of her every movement. If she doesn't want any nearby male to approach, she keeps her shoes on and covers her body with more than her clothing. But, rest assured, any time a woman reveals more of herself to you, it's no accident. She wants you to come over.

UNDERCOVER SEX SIGNAL #6:

The Exposé

Here, you might think that Ashley isn't noticing you and is oblivious to the fact that her dress is falling off. No way! Ashley is exquisitely aware of every square millimeter of skin she's showing. In her mind, she is giving you one strong come-on. Often, a woman will wait until she knows you're looking and then strategically let her dress fall off of one shoulder. Or pull her blouse or T-shirt open to reveal more skin. What other sex signal do you spot in this photo?

You could take your cue from her for an opener and, perhaps loosening your collar, say something like; "It is warm in here, isn't it?" That shows her you haven't been oblivious to her overtly sexual signal but at the same time you aren't being rude. She will like that.

UNDERCOVER SEX SIGNAL #7:

The Sole-Bearing Shoe Dangle

Practically the only time that baring more flesh can truly be subconscious is when a woman lets a shoe dangle on the end of her toes. Be on the lookout for her jiggling it, as that can be indicative of positive sexual energy. Letting one of her shoes actually fall to the floor is sometimes used as a come-on. If a woman lets a shoe fall nearby, be sure to make a nosedive for it; then hold it like a loyal footman replacing Cinderella's slipper. Corny? Perhaps. But she'll soon elevate you to Prince Charming in her book.

Serious Science (and Big Money) Gets into the Act

Interestingly enough, when it comes to finally unraveling what romantic attraction is all about, the National Science Foundation turned out to be the heavyweight champion. When officials at the venerable NSF decided to give a modest $84,000 grant to two women to explore the subject of romance, they had no idea they'd be taking a finger out of the dyke in the dam and letting floods of studies about love and sex gush in.

The findings of the grant recipients, Ellen Berschied and Elaine Hatfield, might have been quietly filed away on a dusty shelf among other never-to-be-read-again studies, had it not been for former U.S. Senator William Proxmire of Wisconsin. When routine news of the NSF grant came across his desk, he started spewing fire and spitting smoke. He shot out a press release accusing the NSF of "meddling where it didn't belong" and ranting that "romance speculations should be left to poets, not scientists." The senator's reaction started a media tornado that Bershied and Hatfield were reluctantly sucked up into. They were catapulted into banner headlines. "Read all about it! Read all about it! NSA blasted for frivolous grant!" Soon, however, everyone was asking, "Yeah, what is romantic love?"

But if leaving love to poets was what Proxmire really wanted, he was shooting himself in the foot . . . because a virtual army of researchers jumped on the love boat. Less camera-shy researchers, hoping to cash in on some of the media hype, started conducting studies on every aspect of romancing. They did studies on such varied subjects as whether the man or the woman usually initiates the break-up,[11] which sex more often commits suicide due to a broken heart,[12] whether you should play "hard to get"[13] and (now here's a worthless bit of information) what type of music makes rats the horniest.[14]

Curious about the answers? They are as follows: (1) women, (2) men, (3) NOT at first (later on it can't hurt) and (4) jazz (if you're a rat, that is, the kind with four legs and a skinny mangy tail).

Most of the wannabe scientific stars that conducted these studies never got their names in newspapers like Berschied and Hatfield, but mankind got a very valuable legacy. Thanks to their research, we now know a whole lot more about attraction and how women communicate their interest sexually.

Thank you, Senator Proxmire.

9

Why They Asked Me to Write This Book

My own research in the area of human sexuality, which formally spanned more than 10 years (and informally has been continuing ever since), drew less political attention but much media attention—including a full page in *Time Magazine* declaring "Sex Fantasy Goes to Broadway."

Soon after college, while still working at other jobs, I founded and directed a research organization called *The Project,* a not-for-profit corporation established to explore relationships and sexuality. My volunteers and I interviewed thousands of individuals and couples on what they wanted in a relationship and how they set about getting it. We asked them about their sexual realities and their sexual fantasies.

We confirmed some interesting facts about women. For example, take the same guy, same face, same bod—and they're more apt to flip for him if they happen to meet him in a "nice" place.[15] They're also more apt to flip for the same guy if he's "well-dressed,"[16] if he jokingly reveals one of his little foibles,[17] and if he maintains strong eye contact when they meet.[18] That doesn't mean you should don your tux to go stare women down in the museum to tell them you pick your toes. It does, however, mean you should heed studies like this that we'll explore and put to good use when dealing with the more perplexing sex.

At *The Project,* we catalogued these and hundreds of other findings about people's sexual habits and then communicated them to the public through the realm of theater. Practically every Thursday, Friday, and Saturday evening for a decade, volunteers and our professional team of performers presented psycho-sexual dramatizations on stage. (And the performers all kept their clothes on!)

After the hour-long performance, I and often some of my colleagues from ASSECT, the American Society of Sex Educators, Counselors and Therapists, or a visiting sex therapist, would conduct a rap session on stage with the audience.

Because this unusual project, which dramatized information about people's deepest sexual longings, had no nudity and no explicit language (*Time Magazine* described it as "squeaky clean"), it caught the attention of many mainstream magazines and the three major television networks. Some of the vignettes were presented on national television. Therefore, even more people the world over called or wrote to *The Project* detailing precisely what they wanted in their relationships and in their sex lives. They told us what they had achieved, or had failed to achieve, in reaching those goals. The letters were fraught with tales of misunderstanding between how the sexes communicate and the anguish it caused.

I read the letters from women with great empathy. Everything they wrote underscored my ever-expanding knowledge of how women are continually exuding sexual hints that men are continually missing. It also confirmed my suspicion that, at other times, a woman will do something in total innocence only to see it misinterpreted.

In a study called "Can Men and Women Differentiate Between Friendly and Sexually Interested Behavior?" approximately 80 men and 80 women were shown films of a male and a female acting in either an innocently friendly or a sexually interested fashion.[19] Men scored very badly on that test. Women were far more perceptive.

This shows that men not only miss sex signals that are genuine but also often see an action as a come-on when it is not! Then they try to pick the woman up and wonder why when she says, "Get lost!" Or the opposite happens. Low self-esteem clouds a man's judgment, and he doesn't approach a woman who would welcome his advances. Either way, he loses.

For example, since different cultures have different "comfort zones" in regard to how close they stand to strangers, an American man would probably think a Latin woman was coming on to him if she stood too close to him by the water cooler at work. So he'd make a pass at the Latin lovely only to get slapped, first with rejection and then with a sexual harassment suit.

The sad thing is that the guy missed out because he never made a pass at another stunner, the Scandinavian sales rep. Why? Because he thought she was giving him the cold shoulder. But all she was doing was backing up into her comfort zone of 3 to 4 feet when he spoke with her.

There are, however, many women who will use proximity as a sex signal. While talking with a man, she may stand a little closer to him than her normal "comfort zone." Or she may invade his. Often a woman will move into a man's zone and see how he reacts.

On the average, people feel uncomfortable if you come more than within 24 inches of their "personal body space"—unless you find them sexually attractive, that is. Women often use this invasion of a man's personal space as a way to announce their availability.

If a woman moves a bit too close to you, it will be on purpose. Then, she'll be watching your reaction very closely. If, when she closes the distance between you, you act surprised in any way, that's a big strike against you. She's bound to misinterpret it and think you're not affectionate and wouldn't be able to give her what she wants in bed. When she moves too close, you *must* reward her aggressive move by a smile or even a slight move forward yourself.

UNDERCOVER SEX SIGNAL #8:

The Close Encounter

Here Jade is fleetingly invading the man's "personal space" as she is getting off the stool. She comes to within 18 inches of Matt's face, if only for a few moments. But, being supersensitive to such signals, she expects him to pick up on it. Matt is reacting perfectly. He smiles and even teasingly pretends he is trapping her in the circle of his arm and his knee. So as not to be too aggressive, he lets her go—but not before the point is made: He's hep to her signals and he wants her.

Like the work of Ellen Berschied and her colleagues, our research project also received a sizable grant, and we were asked to bring our message of sexual loneliness and miscommunication to the public by creating a Broadway show based on *The Project*. After much work and horrendous but hilarious theatrical gaffs, we opened our show, called *Another Way to Love*, to packed houses at the old Bijou Theater on Broadway. I didn't mind (much) when the critics panned the show from a theatrical standpoint, because they applauded our rare research on subliminal sexuality and comprehension of the sexual signals people exude.

Now, as a consultant and motivational speaker in the field of communications, my particular specialty is the plethora of quicksilver subliminal signals that are exchanged between people, such as, for example between a vendor and a buyer, a boss and an employee, jury members and an attorney, etc. But the exchanges that I find most intriguing are the signals cast between a man and a woman who might potentially be lovers. And that, gentlemen, is what *U.S.S.* is all about—reading a woman's signals to win her heart, mind, and body.

Men Looking for Love—and Sex— in All the Wrong Ways

I've been almost constantly on the road in the past several years, speaking or consulting during the days. But in the evenings, I turn into a bird-watcher in hot pursuit of a rare species called "lovebirds who do it right." I've sat perched in hundreds of restaurants, hotel cocktail lounges, and pubs watching the human ballet of men and women looking for love, mostly in all the wrong ways.

There's rarely an exception to the rule. When I observe a man picking up correctly on a woman's undercover signals before he makes an approach, he is usually successful. When he responds well to her signals during the conversation, the two of them stay together throughout the entire evening. Many of them leave together.

But if the male begins to deviate from what the studies prove works, I see the woman starting to lose interest. And unless he quickly jumps back on track, the lady usually makes her sentiments quite clear. While spying on their interaction, I can often pinpoint the precise moment and the exact move that "disqualified" the guy in her estimation.

Men are more forgiving if they like a woman's looks. (She blew her nose on the dinner napkin? No problem. She's got great tits. She bumped into someone and didn't say, "Excuse me?" No problem. Great ass.) But we females make brutal snap judgments on the flimsiest evidence. It's sad, because often we're the big losers. If an otherwise terrific guy makes one King Dork move when meeting a woman, she's likely to write him off before she ever gets to know him. Please understand, we want you gentlemen to notice us—but to be cool about it. That's one of the reasons I wrote the book.

As part of my research, I ordered a truckload of books for men on how to meet and make it with women. The guys in Amazon. com's mailroom must have loved that day. When the books were dumped on my doorstep, I discovered that most of the publishers had squashed more baloney between the covers of their books than the world-famous Katz's Deli squashes corned beef between slices of rye. Many of them were filled with platitudes and "great opening lines" that would only work on an 80-year-old nymphomaniac— when she was drunk. Others offered ivory-tower theories and fuzzy "new-age" advice about the fair sex. Then, of course, there was the usual assortment of books written by the elastic-facts guys who brag they could seduce any woman, anytime, anywhere. To be fair, there were a couple of good books, such as *How to Succeed With Women* (Copeland and Lewis), *Biology of Love* (Perper), *Maxim's Unauthorized Guide*, and, of course, *How to Make Anyone Fall in Love With You* (Lowndes).

Every woman is different. Every man is different. And every situation is different. Taking all this into consideration, *Undercover Sex Signals* gives you the latest information available about the human female and her strange, subtle ways of signaling men. You'll read dozens of tips not found anywhere else to help you meet and form meaningful relationships with women. (Hey, maybe a meaningful relationship for you is a quickie in the back of your Ford pickup. So be it. *U.S.S.* helps there too, but the author hopes you're reading this for something more significant than that.) Whatever your goal with women may be, *Undercover Sex Signals* gives you your best shot . . . because it is the result of scrupulous personal research and observations and of studies and experimentation conducted by serious sociologists. *Undercover Sex Signals* can give you all the proven best moves to make when trying to pick up a woman. But it's up to you to execute them skillfully.

Go for it!

10

I Love Women!

In addition to thinking like a man, I have one other quality in common with guys. I love to be surrounded by beautiful women—tall ones, short ones, shapely in-between ones, blondes, brunettes, redheads, and even an occasional silver-head if her odometer has been set back by diet, exercise, and maybe a little surgery thrown in for good measurements. Don't get me wrong. There's not a lesbian bone in my body. I like to look at women, not sleep with them.

And here's something else I like to do with women that some of you men don't. I like to *listen* to them. And they love to talk to me, because they know I'm giving them good ballsy advice that their other friends don't know how to dish.

Speaking of dishes, those are the ones I've listened to most, which, in addition to the research and books I've written on communications and love, forms my credentials for writing *Undercover Sex Signals*.

While working with *The Project*, and before I decided to go back to school to tack a few more initials on my name, I was an international flight attendant, a model, an actress, and finally the owner of a modeling agency. In addition to my honorary Ph.D. awarded for my life's work in the field of interpersonal communications, I have been soul sister to hundreds of exquisitely beautiful women who have shared their secrets with me—the secrets I now share with you.

The first time I soared with stunning women was as a flight attendant with Pan American (and that was in the days when Weight Watchers drop-outs and kindly old grandmothers couldn't get the job). I learned a lot about my sisters during the long layovers in the outskirts of cities like Monrovia, Liberia, where there was nothing to do but talk the night away to the sound of whirring fans. We weren't permitted to go outside after dark because of the mosquito infestation (not to mention the lion, leopard, and snake infestations). The tales the girls told me about their affairs were as long as Monrovian nights, and most were a lot hotter.

After a couple of years (and a couple of roommates whose plane tragically flew into a mountain top), I landed a safer job, as a fashion model for New York's exclusive Wilhilmina agency, and moved into a high-rise building on the upper east side of New York City that had a singles bar called "Thursday's" on the first floor. My new roommate turned out to be a lingerie model named Jessica who had the same name and frame as the gorgeous toon in "Who Framed Roger Rabbit?" She had the best body I had ever seen in 3-D or 2-D.

Most evenings, after she'd had a long hard day in the showrooms, Jessica and I would go down to Thursday's for the free drinks and munchies the management gave us. The manager there was no fool. He knew that half his male customers patronized Thursday's just to get a glance of Jessica slithering in, hips swirling with more motion than the ocean, nose in the air, just as if she were on the runway. No highway crash ever rivaled the amount of rubbernecking that followed Jessica wherever she went. When she arrived, every man's eyes widened in excitement and every woman's narrowed into green slits of jealousy. I wanted, more than once, to shout, "Bartender! A saucer of milk for every woman in the house, please."

During those years, I learned a lot about how women entice a man to come over and talk to them (and make him think it was his own idea afterward). I also learned the ways a woman signals a man she is talking to that she likes him. Often, the way she does it is

UNDERCOVER SEX SIGNAL # 9:

The Space Invasion

A woman is extremely conscious of how close to a man she is standing or sitting or how close to him she is moving any part of her body or any object. Often, instead of invading his personal bubble of space with her body, she will let her hand, a knee, or an object of hers penetrate his unspoken territory. Here Ashley is not touching the man, but she is letting her arm and hand stay close to him. If a woman makes any similar moves while talking with you, make sure your reaction is one of pleasure. Otherwise, she'll pull back and the relationship can grow more distant.

subtle and has to do with "personal space." Jade demonstrated how a woman is expressing availability when she moves into a man's personal space. There is another way that many women hint at this without actually moving their full bodies into a man's "territory." Everyone in North America, on the average, has a 24-inch imaginary bubble of comfortable body space around him within which no one but close friends or lovers can enter comfortably. As if oblivious to what they are doing, women move a leg, or even an object, such as an ashtray or a bowl of peanuts, into the man's "bubble."

Just as the excitement escalates and everything becomes critical when a football game goes into overtime, your every move in the mating game becomes critical once the touch has been initiated. Other than for shaking hands, you must, unfortunately, let her make the first move when it comes to touching. And usually she will. She will pretend it's unconscious at first. Maybe she'll touch your arm when you make a joke, hold your wrist while pretending she needs to look at your watch, or let her foot "unconsciously" touch your leg. Understand there is nothing inadvertent about this at all. It is a calculated, contrived, carefully planned test to see how you react.

How should you respond? With a smile, a move toward her, and possibly with a reciprocating touch of your own. Just let her know you noticed—and you like it.

UNDERCOVER SEX SIGNAL #10:

The "Innocent" Touch

A woman will never touch you if she doesn't welcome your advances. When she does, you must react warmly and appreciatively. Otherwise, she figures you are either (1) a cold fish not capable of giving a guppy a run for her money or (2) someone who simply doesn't like her, either or both of which will immediately qualify you for her quit list. If a woman does reach out and touch you for any reason—say to take a piece of lint off your jacket, to look at your tie or watch, or as an unconscious gesture after you've cracked a joke—you *must* react very positively. Otherwise, she will feel she's gone too far and will back down.

UNDERCOVER SEX SIGNAL #11:

The Lean-2-U

In some situations, it is not feasible or appropriate for a woman to touch a man or enter his personal zone. In these cases, her tactic will be to lean forward toward him. Never, ever back up when she does this. What other signals do you notice in this photo?

During those years, I enjoyed talking with Jessica and the other models about their boyfriend woes and their sexual frustrations. Most men are as lost as a goose in a snowstorm when it comes to a babe's body. I learned the honest answers to some questions, answers men never get because women always lie to save their egos. But, never fear, all will be revealed in *U.S.S.*

What I didn't enjoy about modeling was the mouse-size diet I had to adhere to to stay employed. I wanted a job that permitted me Pringles at parties and an occasional pig-out on chocolate. It seems the natural career path of burned-out or bummed-out hungry models was to take a crack at acting, which is precisely what I did.

Now I got stories from hundreds of actresses: From Broadway stars to off-off-off-Broadway babies, from Rockettes to *Playboy* pets. The audition lines in theaters all over New York provided the perfect venue for girl talk. There was something about the long afternoon waits in darkened theaters for the producer to shout "NEEEXT" that made us share our deepest secrets about men with one another.

Just to quickly wrap up this autobiography (which is even beginning to bore me), let's cut to the quick and see how my experiences continued to build toward my background for writing *Undercover Sex Signals*. Jobs were tight then, and just a B.A. and no business experience made me a bum bet for any employer. So I went into business for myself. Naturally, I opened a business in which I would still be surrounded by female pulchritude—a "real people" modeling agency and production company, creating shows for cruise ships. Especially on those long cruises, I still had a bevy of beauties bending my ear and asking my advice.

I now conduct corporate seminars on communications skills and, even more fun, public seminars on relationships. At every relationships session, I distribute blank pink cards to the women and blue ones to the men for "questions you've always wanted to ask the opposite sex but were afraid to ask." Right after the break, I collect the cards and read them aloud. The men answer the pink-card questions and the women answer the blue questions—sometimes *very* blue questions. Their unexpurgated answers are yet another source for the candid and accurate data in this book.

So, if you heed *Undercover Sex Signals*, I promise you'll never look at a woman again and wonder if you're going to be shot down. You will see her interest in you as clearly as your fantasies of good times to come.

11

How to Rejection-Proof Yourself

Compared to other professions, the sales profession has one of the highest dropout rates in the first couple of years. Why? There are two big reasons: (1) the fear of rejection and (2) abhorrence of cold calls. Beware, such fears in big-dame hunting can blow you out of the water and make you never want to get your feet wet again.

Are you one of those guys who, when they go to a party, set their sights on the best-looking fox in the place and never get up the courage to take a shot at her? If so, you probably spend the whole time trying to come up with some opening salvo, and, by the time you've rehearsed it a dozen times, a huddle of jocks has her barricaded. So instead of targeting some other attractive woman who has been signaling *you* all evening, you slump off the field feeling like a failure. Later that evening at home, you thumb or click desperately through the personals and ask yourself, "What's wrong with this picture?"

Many men figure that only the guys with great abs, flashy wheels, and thick shiny manes of black hair flowing down their well-toned backs can make it with those women. Wrong. My dentist, Dr. Dan, scores at every party he goes to. (Yes, you heard right, my *dentist*. And he bears a strong resemblance to an albino seal. I'll reveal the secret of his success later.)

Well, what if you never had to fear rejection again? What if *every* woman you approached was eager for your attention? What if *every* time you went to a gathering of any sort, you could leave with a gal on your arm or her phone number in your pocket? What if lots of times you never even needed to go home—to *yours*, that is?

The secret, as you now know, lies in detecting her undercover sex signals. *U.S.S.* will provide you with a detailed map of the female terrain—and tell you what it *indicates* when she squiggles, caresses, or displays this or that part of her body.

However, a simple laundry list of body language, as some books have attempted to provide, is not enough. Nor is such a list accurate. As I said, you must look for "gesture clusters" and view them within the framework of the situation and the presumed personality of the woman emitting them. In this context, no book is large enough to contain them all. Only when you comprehend what causes U.S.S.s and how they manifest themselves will you be able to recognize them on the fly quickly enough to make two people very happy—you *and* the gal who flashed them at you.

Some of them are very subtle—so subtle that a quick flick of the wrist can mean the difference between "Come up and see me sometime" and "Get outta my face!" For example, a woman's hands are an accurate indication of precisely how much she likes you at any particular time. Just like a weathervane, her hands turn toward you when her warmth is blowing in your direction—and away from you when she's blowing cold.

UNDERCOVER SEX SIGNAL #12:

Weathervane Palm

This is affectionately referred to by those who are savvy to undercover sex signals as "the old wrist flash." When a woman looks at you while resting her chin on her knuckles, palm forward, it means she likes your style. It suggests she is saying, "I submit" or "I accept you."

Here Jade, in the exact same position but with her *knuckles* forward, says, "This is not a fist…*yet*! Beat it!"

Some people consider the palms to be very sensual parts of the body because they are usually hidden. I mean, when was the last time you actively remember seeing someone's palms? Other than the beggar's on the corner, that is. Or those of the female impersonator in that comedy show giving "the limp wrist." Pretty forgettable, huh?

In the first photo, Jade was open to your attentions. But with a simple turn of her wrists, she cut off your approach. If you are already in conversation with a woman and she turns her palms toward you, it means she is warming up to you and likes you. If her palms are open when you start speaking with her but then turn to a knuckles forward position, watch out. This is more indicative of a protective, possibly even hostile, feeling.

If you haven't made her acquaintance yet and she flashes her palms at you across the room, it signals that she would like you to "Come hither." As you start to walk toward her, keep her palms in the edge of your sight. They're like a weathervane in the wind indicating her interest. If they start to turn away, slow down, back up a bit, give her a smile, and watch her palms to see if she's up for a second try.

But don't jump to conclusions too quickly. There is another possibility. Maybe she is quite attracted to you but your attention makes her as shy as a mail-order bride. So her hands tense up. It's like the airplane travelers who clench their fists on take-off and landing so the rest of their body can appear at ease. (Flight attendants call them "the white knucklers.")

If you suspect that positive sexual tension, not rejection, has occasioned this reaction, look for some of the other undercover sex signals that we will explore. If she is not giving you other U.S.S.s and her closed fist is accompanied by other signs of rejection, such as averted eyes, crossed arms, or turning away, you're playing with a cold deck and it's time to cash in the chips with that particular gal.

Proof of U.S.S.s (and Why Men Miss Them)

12

Most Potential Lovers Never Even Meet

Back in 1982, a guy named John Andrew Jones wrote his thesis on what clinicians call "the proceptive female", (and what other women call "the aggressive bitch"). His thesis, *Nonverbal Flirtation Behavior: An Observational Study in Bar Settings,* got him his master's degree. (Cool! He got away with sitting on bar stools at the local speakeasy, ogling women, secretly whispering notes into his little tape recorder, and then compiling his notes for his thesis.)[20]

Jones noted that whenever a man and a woman started talking, the female made the first move, albeit subtle, more than half the time. Often, a woman would look at the man and then quickly look away as though embarrassed to have been caught glancing his way. In the split second it took for the man to feel her eyes and look at her, she was now looking down. He, probably feeling he didn't pass muster, would also look away. But inevitably she would take a quick peek back to see if he was now giving her the eye. Alas, because of the reason just cited, he wasn't looking at her. This would disappoint her. Her disappointment soon turned to disinterest.

Repeatedly, at parties, in restaurants, in museums, in shopping malls, and indeed, almost everywhere men and women gather, I've seen this same ballet of the eyeballs performed. It usually has a sad ending, each thinking the other is disinterested and neither having the confidence or tenacity to keep the dance progressing toward a meeting.

Nine times out of ten, the reason you don't meet a chick you're interested in is due to faulty eye contact. If you catch her eye on the street, do NOT look away. She will take it as a sign that you are not interested. If you lock eyeballs at a party and she looks away, do NOT make the same mistake. Smile and keep your baby blues, browns, or greens right on her.

> Since a chick's mind is going around as fast as beaters on an electric mixer when she sees you, get in her line of sight and let her size up your looks before you approach. That way, you get a reading on how much she likes you and she'll be more relaxed when talking with you.

It Takes a Woman to Know a Woman

Since 1983, there have been even more dramatic studies on women and their naturally aggressive nature. Monica Moore, a university professor, proved that the figure was not just one-half, as John Andrews had calculated. She observed that the female initiated two-thirds of the male/female "pick-ups." (There is speculation that because Ms. Moore was a woman, she was able to recognize signals that even randy rubbernecking male researchers missed— and that the figure had been two-thirds all along. It takes one to know one.)

In her landmark study called *Nonverbal Courtship Patterns in Women*, Ms. Moore embedded hidden cameras in the ceiling of a large singles' event with about 200 women and 200 men in attendance.[21] She filmed the entire party from above. The film tracked who approached whom, who danced with whom, who left with whom, etc. Afterward, she played the tape for her assistants. Each time they spotted a male approaching a female to dance or speak with her, they rewound the tape and analyzed the encounter from its inception.

The results of her study? Two out of every three times a guy came over to talk to a girl, she had subliminally lured him over with one subtle signal or another. Although the subjects were relatively young women of college age, they had already mastered the art of the undercover sex signal.

However, it doesn't take a B.A. to sling out U.S.S.s. A hot female chimpanzee will spot a cool-dude chimp, stroll toward him, gracefully (for a monkey) turn around, and then tip her buttocks toward his nose so he gets a whiff of her wazoo. He thumps the ground in pleasure and goes after her.[22]

Are you assuming the female of our more evolved species is above that? Think again. Another Monica in our history, Monica Lewinsky, wearing a thong instead of panties under her skirt, flashed her bare ass at then-President Clinton. Thump, thump, he made a monkey of himself too.

A great ploy is going to places where men are *supposed* to be helpless and look helpless. If a chick doesn't take pity on you and offer her help, ask for it. In the supermarket (women love men who cook), you might ask her for example, "Uh, excuse me, do you know if this mango has to be cooked before eating?" In the laundromat (women also adore men who do their own laundry), you might say, for example, "Gosh, do you think it's OK if I put this red T-shirt in with my white dress shirts?"

Back to Ms. Moore's bash. What types of undercover sex signals had the women used to lure the men? More than one-fourth of

UNDERCOVER SEX SIGNAL #13:

The Necking

When two foxes are fighting in the wild, the loser bares his neck to say, "I submit." And when a female fox like Tanya here bares hers, it expresses her vulnerability or openness to the male. She becomes very animated and, at one point, lifts her hair high off her neck, sending a strong message to her partner. Your compliment on her beautiful hair would be playing the game well.

UNDERCOVER SEX SIGNAL #14:

The Underarm Flash

A woman's underarms are rarely seen, so exposing them to you is "special" for her. She is quite conscious that she is leaning back, supposedly appearing relaxed. But she knows precisely what she is doing. To play the game well, you might wink at her and say, "I wish I had a feather."

them had smiled at the targeted man—offering just a tiny smile (you've got to keep your eyes out, guys)—before *he* got the idea to make the approach. Since there was music, many a woman swayed alone to the beat while keeping eye contact with her chosen male. Moore and her team spotted dozens of other man-baiting gestures, such as women tossing their hair, touching their exposed necks, and caressing their own arms or thighs during eye contact.

UNDERCOVER SEX SIGNAL #15:

The Lips Lick

Here Sandy is issuing a very primitive and bold invitation that almost borders on lecherous. A woman will lick her lips either conspicuously or covertly for several reasons. One is that she wants to make her lips look moist and more inviting to you. Another is that she is thinking about intimacy with you and is licking her lips for her own pleasure. A third is that she is trying to tantalize you with what treats might be in store for you from her lips.

In Monica Moore's study, the bolder women licked their lips while staring into the eyes of the man they wanted. A few women paraded past the man, brazenly swinging their hips, and then looked back to make sure he noticed. Several even "accidentally" bumped into poor unsuspecting males who were seated around the room. And some of *those* guys didn't even get it! Duh.

Gentlemen, it bears repeating again. *Nothing* with a woman is accidental. A woman notices every man who walks into a room. You walked in? She's sized you up. Period. End of story. And if a female does anything at all to make you notice her, that means she's interested. Unfortunately for you, however, if you don't bite immediately and appropriately, she goes on to more interested and interesting game.

Once, in a jazz club called the Blue Note, I spotted a man who was as smooth as silk and decided to throw him a few undercover sex signals—purely for research, of course. I kept my eyes right on him. I suppose that, eventually, he felt my eyeballs drilling a crater into the side of his head, because he looked over.

The women in Monica Moore's study had a good batting average with the lipstick ploy, so I tossed my hair and went diving into my purse. I had recently read a study in the respected *Journal of Social Psychology* called "Lipstick as a Determiner of First Impressions of Personality," revealing that, when it comes to color of lipstick, a majority of males prefer a good clear red.[23] I extracted the red stick of dynamite from my bag and exposed the wick.

I waited for him to look back. When he did, I lifted the lipstick to my lips and lowered my compact mirror to maintain unbroken eye contact with him. Then I slowly circled my lips in bright red. As a final kiss on the trick, I pressed my lips together to smooth out the lipstick and then wetted them by running my tongue around them, slowly, sensuously, all the while maintaining a direct gaze.

A woman doesn't need to read 21st-century sex manuals to know that full wet red lips are very sexy. More than 5,000 years ago, B.C., babes dressed in bearskin began rubbing red into their lips. Why? They were no "dummies." They knew that when sexually aroused, more blood flows to the lips and makes them bigger and redder.

Cut to today. A New Mexico State University psychologist, Victor Johnston, is currently attempting to prove the drawing

UNDERCOVER SEX SIGNAL #16:

The Primp

If a woman likes you, she will primp by putting on lipstick, powdering her nose, or combing her hair to make you aware of her appearance. If you haven't met her yet, she can use this as bait to draw you across the room. If you have met her and, let's say, you are on a dinner date with her, check to see when you've returned from a temporary absence (to use the phone, the men's room, etc.) whether she has done any secret primping. If she has, it's an excellent sign that she cares about you enough to look her very best.

power of big lips by using a computer program called FacePrints, which generates 30 facial images. Volunteers in the study rate the faces for beauty on a scale of 1 to 9. The results? Thus far, both men and women seem to think big lips on the opposite sex are more attractive and sensual.

Keep your eyes out for any woman who is primping. It could mean that she is putting on the war paint to attract you in particular. Or maybe it merely indicates she is "looking." In either case, your odds are better with a primping woman.

It also provides you with an excellent opportunity for the perfect opening line. Casually comment, "You don't need any of that" . . . implying that she is already attractive enough.

My Blue Note ploy went off like clockwork. My big smile with freshly painted red lips lured him over as soon as the musicians took a break. Scott, as I later found his name to be, asked me if we had met.

"You know, that's precisely what I was thinking," I lied.

One thing led to another, and we went out a few times. On one of our later dates, feigning forgetfulness, I asked him how we had met. "Oh," he said, with a verbal swagger, "I spotted you at the Blue Note and came right over and introduced myself." When men take ownership of a good idea at work, women bare their fangs in anger. But when they want to retroactively take ownership of making the approach, women reveal their pearly whites in a sly smile that lies, "Of course you did, dear."

Blessed be the lies that bind.

You probably aren't aware of it, but you have most likely already dated a few women who had been casting you undercover sex signals. But, as was the case with Scott, your male ego may have conveniently helped you forget that it wasn't you who initiated the meeting. Just think how much more successful you'll be when you become hep to her signals.

Some Surprising Facts About Women and U.S.S.s

13

Are U.S.S.s Nature or Nurture?

To begin our exploration, let us turn to our furry little friends. Researchers conducted an experiment called "Parental Behavior in the Mongolian Gerbil," which sounds as exciting as working a tollbooth. They confirmed their findings with others using rats and rabbits. (They evidently chose ones that are just about as randy as single guys.)

The research team proved repeatedly that it is the *interaction*, not just the female's "come-on" that results in copulation.[24] The guy gerbil had to respond appropriately, according to Miss Gerbil, for her to flash gerbil-ass at him. If he got ahead of the game and exposed his, uh, gerbil penis to her in a lewd fashion prematurely, she might shun him. She might do the same if he tried to jump her fragile little bones too quickly. The *artistry* with which he played the game determined whether the guy gerbil got laid or not.

And so it is with our supposedly more evolved species. Let's return, momentarily to the question of nature vs. nurture. Guy and girl gerbils have no culture to teach them how to behave. They have no symbols, no language to communicate or dictate their actions. And, insofar as we know, they seem to have no minds or intelligence for remembering what should and should not be done. They are simply run by their own biological needs. (Does that sound like any of your buddies?) Therefore, even with gerbils, sex with a desired partner is often not consummated. (Can you identify with that?)

As we work our way up the mammal chain to humans, the matter becomes even more confusing. Not only must guy humans send out the right signals in response to those of the females, but also they must emit the right signals for each particular lady AND be able to read them in the context of her culture, his culture, and what they've both been taught works. It's a mighty complicated process to consummate a simple biological act. But not to worry. You're being talked through it, systematically.

Graduating from gerbils to gals, the worlds of science and sociology agree that there is a strong thread of nature in a woman's sex signals. But her signals are, unlike those of the gerbil, complicated due to an organ she has that gerbils don't—a brain.

14

Are Her Sex Signals
Conscious or Unconscious?

This brings us to the question of whether or not she knows she's sending out U.S.S.s. Sometimes, she does; at other times, she doesn't. We have said that if your looks, for a reason we'll explore later, happen to "push her buttons," she might squiggle, caress herself, or expose more of her skin. Why?

It comes from internal stimulation. Every red-blooded male when he comes of age should be informed that a female's pleasure center is spread all over her body, whereas his is more localized. For example, a woman's body feels good all over when you kiss her neck, caress her arms or legs, nuzzle her thighs, or massage her feet. So, when she gets a gander at a man she likes, her body becomes tingly, head to toe, and she starts the job herself.

At first, when she's very young, this happens unconsciously. You've probably seen little girls sitting on Daddy's lap squealing with delight, squirming all over, laughing and running their hands through their hair. (Conversely, guys, when you got excited on Mommy's lap, you grabbed your little pecker and got your hand slapped.)

Grown-up girls, at least the smart ones, notice that certain men respond positively to such self-caressing moves. They like that.

That's when their sex signals shift from unconscious to conscious. The really smart women practice and perfect them to have an even more magnetic effect on men. A lady's signals can become so calculated and precise that using them becomes an art form. She learns to emit each signal with the intensity she wishes to convey.

UNDERCOVER SEX SIGNAL #17:

The Hair Play

If you are talking with a woman and she begins to play with her hair, it is a subconscious (at first) wish that you were touching her. If you respond well, her wish becomes conscious and she begins to use the signal as a come-on. It is a sign of either excess sexual nervousness or her trying to tantalize a man into imagining that he is playing with her hair. Depending on the woman's mood, women with long hair often let it swing over one eye to attain the peekaboo effect or to appear glamorous à la Lauren Bacall. One of the most popular ways a woman uses her hair as a come-on is to give it a flip while looking at the man.

15

Cupid Does Drugs
(or What Happens When the Bug Bites Her)

There is probably not a man alive who hasn't said about a woman he's loved and lost, "What did she see in *him*?" Well, we found out what makes a woman want to strip down when she sees one guy and zip up when spotting another. Surprise, surprise, it all goes back to drugs. In this case, I'm talking about a drug mightier than marijuana and stronger than Singapore slings. And, no, you can't buy it on the street.

It's the chemical Mother Nature injects into the little lady's system when she sees a guy who sets off just the right series of neurological responses. This reaction usually only occurs when the woman is confronted with a guy who, for esoteric reasons, rings her bells, or who looks like Tom Cruise or Kevin Costner. (I told you Mother Nature's no fool.)

If, however, you're more of a Jack Palance in the looks department, you can still score with her by getting Mother Nature on your side. But there's a catch. First, we have to go back to chemistry class to understand precisely what happens in her body when she goes berserk over a guy. (In fact, you're not immune to it either. The same thing happens to you when the "L" word tries to enter your vocabulary.)

> Speaking of the "L" word, don't use it too quickly with chicks. They won't trust you. Instead, say something like "You're the most unique woman I've ever met." She'll noodle over that one for days.

After the Proxmire media hurricane about the National Science Foundation and the large grant blew over, scads of scientists put their pointed little heads together and conducted hundreds of experiments on sex, love, and romance.

The following is the absolute truth and nothing but the truth, as promised, about love and desire. There's nothing touchy-feely about it. The explanation will satisfy even the most organized guy brain—even you guys who iron your boxer shorts, fold your socks before putting them in the drawer, and alphabetize your canned veggies in the cupboard.

Here's the scoop. Researchers asked women how they felt when they looked at a guy they really liked. The women answered, "Well, my heart beats faster." "My palms get sweaty." "My throat gets dry, and my body gets tingly," "My skin feels all prickly," etc. Most replied, "I feel all funny inside" or "It's chemistry."

UNDERCOVER SEX SIGNAL #18:

The Self-Caress

Ashley is obviously feeling a tingling sensation in her body. If she were younger and less experienced, caressing her own body might just be instinctive, like scratching an itch. When she became a beautiful woman, she recognized that men enjoyed watching her caress herself. Now it is used as self-fulfillment and a way to lure you over to talk with her.

"Hmm," scientists started thinking. "That sounds suspiciously like a reaction to amphetamines." Could it possibly be that love, that sacred emotion in the words of Robert Burns, "Love, O lyric Love, half angel and half bird? And all a wonder and a wild desire," was just *drugs*? A chemical reaction?

Well, I have good news and bad news here. The bad news, especially for romantics reading this, is that her deciding to drop cotton for you is pretty much a chemical reaction. But not to worry. The good news is that, even though it's difficult to sway her emotions, I'm going to give you a way to get some of the sexy chemicals running through her system when she sees you.

> Parallel parking naked with you for the first time is a much, much, much bigger deal for her than it is for you. Undress her slowly. Tell her how beautiful her body is each step of the way. And let her know how special a night it is for you. Otherwise, you risk losing your license with her.

Thanks to a principle in the world of psychiatry called "cognitive consistency," when we find our bodies reacting in a certain way, our emotions follow.

> *Cognitive consistency says that individuals strive to keep their cognition psychologically consistent and that when inconsistencies do arise they strive to restore consistency.*[25]

So, if her body gets all prickly when she gets a gander of you, she will probably fool herself into believing that it's her heart that is responding. And, as always with women, wherever her heart goes, the body follows.

Scientists have now isolated the very structure of the chemical at the core of her little heart's going pitty-pat. It is quite similar to amphetamines except that it is naturally produced. If something familiar or exciting strikes a woman when looking into your baby blues, WHOOOSH! She's swept away as though on a drug and becomes very high on you.

Like any drug, this amphetamine-type substance causes different reactions in different women. Some freeze like a deer in headlights and are practically unable to speak or move. Others, like Ashley, begin to caress themselves to counterbalance the tingling

UNDERCOVER SEX SIGNAL #19:

The Shoulder Scrunch

Some women, especially the more spontaneous and free-spirited ones, will allow themselves to become like a kid again when in the company of a man they enjoy. They may scrunch their shoulders, move their breasts enticingly, and become wide-eyed. Much of it is in direct response to the phenylethylamine flowing through their systems. She is also using another sex signal with her right hand, which you will learn shortly.

sensation. And still others have the opposite reaction. They become silly or scrunch up their shoulders in delight.

Scientists who study depression and elation have recently made remarkable discoveries about chemicals in the human brain called neurotransmitters. We now know that they are responsible for that crazy wonderful feeling that made Romeo OD and Gene Kelly sing in the rain.

Now the mother of neurotransmitters, the one that really causes grown men and women to come unglued and fall off their hinges, can be identified specifically as the one called phenylethylamine (PEA).[26] The way PEA affects us is this: The brain is divided into separate parts and, in total, is about the size of a grapefruit (although when someone is infatuated, the description PEA-brained would be accurate on two counts).

The first part is just above the spinal cord and guides such instincts as survival, territoriality, etc. (By the way, if details put your feet to sleep, you can skip to the bottom of the page. If you're one of those guys who like to know the reason for everything (or a trivia fanatic), read on. The next part, the *limbic system*, controls such emotions as anger, despondency, hate, and, conversely, calm, happiness, and love. The third section, the *cortex*, is the part that looks like a ball of spaghetti-length macaroni and comes to mind when we think, "brain." This part is responsible for our thoughts.[27]

The three parts communicate with one another through a hundred billion impulses (give or take a few billion with certain people) going from neuron to neuron. PEA lies at the end of some cells to help the impulses jump from one neuron to another. But here's the problem: The substance itself, PEA, is a natural amphetamine that gets you high. So, when you see someone who rings your bell, your PEA-manufacturing system generates more product; thus, more PEA floods through all parts of the brain—including the rational thinking part. So, not only do you have an escalation in your sense of territoriality about the love object, but also your limbic system makes you feel ecstatically happy (or dreadfully miserable, depending on the circumstances).

Welcome back, 90 percent of readers. As I explained above, a person's "think box" gets all unwired by this naturally produced drug. So does the body. That's one of the reasons why, when a woman spots you and likes you, her body begins to twitch, itch, or squiggle. That's the "nature" part of her signals. As she grows a little older, she is often embarrassed and tries to hide them. But when you become a U.S.S. expert, you'll even recognize her repressed signals.

Be on the Lookout for Her "Semi-Signals"

Many women are probably attracted to you who don't feel comfortable overtly casting you a signal. Society frowns on it, and they don't want you to think they are too aggressive. Therefore, you must be on the lookout for "incipient," "indicated," or "aborted" sex signals.

These are signals that a woman started to give but, due to shyness or not wanting to be caught giving you the come-on, aborted. She might start to caress an object or herself, but then stop. She might start to loosen her clothing or mirror your movements, but then stop. She might just fleetingly flash her palm, dangle a shoe, or run her fingers through her hair—so quick you'd hardly see it. It pays to train your eyes to catch her in the act and reward her actions with a warm smile.

She Wants You to Play the Game Too

Because a woman expects that you will pick up on subtle signals, she expects you to do your part and play the game too. Her interest quickly dwindles if you just stand around and drool. You must respond to each of her signals appropriately in order to encourage her next volley.

I heard you ask, "What would be appropriate in this case?" Maybe an ever-so-fleeting glance at her hand and then a warm smile. Or maybe your nonchalantly keeping your eyes on her hand as it circles the rim, then looking away as if you hadn't noticed, and finally turning your head and giving her a smile. Maybe even a wink.

What kinds of moves can you make if you're on a date and having dinner with her? Well, you could slide your wine glass up next to hers, for example. You could begin caressing your glass, mirroring her movements while maintaining eye contact. You could look a little too long at her hands running around the glass and then give her a smile. There are any number of ways to play it and all of them work as long as they are subtle, respectful, not suggestive—and fun!

> Your playing the game of sex signals with her can be compared to a game of tennis. No top player wants to fool around with a mediocre one. But if you manage a great serve and return her volley with a nice slice, she will definitely want to play with you. Be mischievous. Be sophisticated. Be fun. Play her game. She started it! Soon you'll develop a sixth sense for the right rejection-proof moves. And the score at the end of the game? She's hoping it will be "Love/Love."

Let's say such a tennis game continues for a while and, if you don't miss a ball, you're soon standing as close to her as a wet T-shirt, your eyes interlocked with hers. The two of you are shutting out the rest of the crowd, chatting, and having a drink together before setting up a date. Then (if all goes well according to Mother Nature's plan), you mate.

Incidentally, it's not just romance that gives you a PEA brain. Why do you think otherwise rational adults jump out of airplanes? One researcher measured the amount of PEA in the real pee of parachute jumpers while in free fall. (I'm trying hard *not* to visualize how he gathered his samples.) He discovered that the PEA levels of the divers' urine soared as they catapulted toward the earth.[28]

Our PEA-soaked lovesick brain causes grown men to talk baby talk and grown women to count the hairs on their lovers' chests (683 the last time I counted) and feel that the dumbest things about their lovers are sacred.

Now this Mickey Finn of romance, this popper of passion that gets the lady temporarily blasted, doesn't last that long—fortunately for her and for you. It's all part of nature's plan. If it lasted, you and the missus would still be singing your love from rooftops and keeping all the neighbors awake—or having sex around the clock when you should be getting the kids ready for school. As a headline read recently in the *International Herald Tribune*, "Love Has an Eighteen Month Expiration Date."[29]

One of the original researchers on this phenomenon, Dorothy Tennov, was a bit more hopeful about *limerance*, the bulky word she coined for that crazy want-to-rip-your-clothes-off-right-now kind of passion. "The most frequent duration," she wrote, "is between approximately 18 months and three years."[30] Mother Nature's no fool. She knows that's as long as it takes to get a male and a female shagging, get her full of heir, and then get the offspring tottering on two feet. Mother Nature doesn't give a spit about what comes after. Broken hearts? Henpecked husbands? Spousal abuse? Long-term happiness in a relationship? "Forget it," says Mother N. "Just hang in there until that little bambino is walking; then you're on your own."

Beware the Female Love Junkies

Having a basic understanding of PEA is crucial both for turning women on and for understanding them. For instance, have you ever known a woman who leaps from one relationship to another? In the light of this newfound knowledge, you would understand that she's hooked on the adrenaline rush that PEA gives her. When the first rush wears off, she jumps to another man who makes her PEA rush all over again. She should have your sympathy, as she is uninformed and sick, She's called a "love junkie," because she needs to keep that initial high going all the time. And, no matter how right two people are for each other, that's not going to happen if she needs that constant jolt. Other love junkies get involved with men who mistreat them to keep the high going.

Unfortunately, many wonderful relationships are destroyed because of ignorance about this chemical reaction in our bodies. A man and woman get nice and comfy in a relationship and when nature takes its course and the PEA subsides, they blame it on the relationship. They think their love is dying instead of understanding that it's just the natural pre-programmed PEA fizzle time. PEA also plays a role in one of the biggest head-scratchers men have about women:

Why Do Women Go for the "Bad Boys"?

The most asked question by men except for "What's a great opening line?" (yes, we'll get to that) is "Why do women seem to go for the bad guys?"

There are several reasons, and many of the rogue-loving women are as confused as you are about their self-destructive liaisons. Even worse, many women don't even admit their perverse preference. They put "trust," "honesty," "respect," and "commitment" at the top of the list, according to an assistant professor of psychology at the University of Winnipeg who asked 141 students to rate the attributes they considered most important in a love relationship. So why is it that the untrustworthy, dishonest guys who have little respect for them and will never commit to a lasting relationship hold such an attraction for so many women? They wind up thinking about them all the time, waiting for them to call, and feeling euphoric when they do and miserable when they don't. And yet this kind of dramatic excitement ended up at the bottom of the list of things the psychology students said they wanted in a relationship.[31]

One of my girlfriends, a self-admitted rogue lover, says the nice guy, the one her mother would simply adore, is too familiar to be sexy. When she's with him, she feels psychologically chaperoned, as if her mother were sitting right next to them. With the rogue, on the other hand, she feels naughty and excited. It reminds her of the time when she was a little girl and could be naughty when Mommy wasn't looking.

The question of why women think they want one type of man and go for another doesn't just baffle the women themselves and the nice guys they'd prefer to be attracted to. Serious researchers have explored this phenomenon and named it "The Stockholm Syndrome."[32] In fact, one researcher even thought he could develop a scale for detecting a woman's tendency to let her heart be tromped on by a rogue. His study, called "A scale for identifying Stockholm Syndrome reactions in young dating women" was published in a professional journal called *Violence and Victims.*[33]

Mother Nature's desire for us to procreate and help our progeny survive and then her callousness to our happiness wouldn't be that bad . . . except for the lag factor. Anthropologists tell us that evolution is notoriously slow and that many young women are dancing to the tune of a different millennium. There was a time in our (by our standards) ancient history when selecting a sensitive, compassionate, loving male would have been a really lamebrained choice. The nice guy would have probably been killed while trying to intellectually reason with the dominant dude in bearskin who held a stone hatchet over his head. And, of course, that would have left the baby with no daddy to go out and bring home the rabbit and fox meat. Mother Nature nudged the primitive pretty and said to her, "Better to go with the powerful jerk, dear." Now the fact that in the 21st century choosing the powerful jerks makes no sense at all hasn't gotten through to some of today's pretty women.

For some severely evolutionarily challenged women, power means hunks that learned how to curl their lips like James Dean or Elvis Presley. For others, it brings to mind big beefcake types like Arnold Schwarzenegger. Power for women who are still evolutionarily challenged but a bit more up-to-date (stuck in, say the last century) is defined as money, possessions, and expensive clothes. Their retarded genes tell them that men with those things are the guys who can take care of them the best. (Unfortunately, a lot of it is pretense—and many of those rich-looking rogues couldn't provide anything more than their own impeccable wardrobes or a gym membership.)

Many women also find abusive men attractive because, to all outward appearances, they seem confident. They give off the air of knowing what they want and pushing others around to get it. Usually it covers up a deep insecurity, but the "tough" guys keep it deeply hidden.

Some women find a perverse pleasure in this type of sometimes near fatal attraction. They miss the drama in their lives that they felt as teenagers They remember the pain, the pleasure, the discovery, and the being on the brink of disaster associated with their first loves. So this type of woman finds the rogue to be exciting. She has no idea what's going to happen next. She could suddenly be having sex with him in a roller coaster at the amusement park or come home to find him in bed with somebody else. That kind of uncertainty gets her juices flowing.[34]

If you find yourself involved with a bad-boy addict, don't become "bad" yourself. Do, however, question the way you act with her. Ask yourself, "Am I doing something too predictable?" Then stamp out all of your unnecessary predictability. Do something to surprise her.

In some cases, the tough guy may remind her of the time she was a little girl. Daddy may have been harsh with her, and so she came to connect such behavior with being cared for. Unfortunately, it's addictive . . . and she may well develop a higher and higher threshold for what it takes to get that adrenaline flowing again. For some, it gets to the point where they have to be abused in order to recapture those melodramatic moments and get their "fix."

The results of a massive study of women who continually chose abusive partners revealed that they suffered low self-esteem and the relationship only aggravated it. The verbal aggression and violence they endured caused depression and a myriad of other symptoms. Yet they stayed. Many were "love dependent," feeling that they could not survive without the partner's love.[35]

It is very common for women who love a bad boy to have a nice guy waiting in the wings—a soft bed to fall on if the tough guy gets too tough. They keep stringing their nice boy along as an insurance policy.

A number of "nice guys" in my seminars ask me if they should stay in the wings in the hope she'll "see the light?" I tell them that the statistics are pretty bleak. She must have a desire to escape the repetitive destructive pattern herself, and, deep down, she probably doesn't want to.

If you should find yourself on the short end of the stick in one of these relationships, it's best just to say, "Girl you've got too much evolutionary baggage!" and walk. (You probably won't get her back with that rejoinder, but it will leave her wondering.)

Secret Is Sexier

Another screwy aspect of attraction related to phenylethylamine became known in a study called "The Allure of Secret Relationships." A resourceful research team was able to survey mixed-sex individuals who played footsie under the table in the presence of their own respective partners The footsie players reported a higher level of obsession with these relationships than with their open ones. It was no mean feat (no pun intended) that the researchers were able to confirm these findings with couples who had had secret relationships in the past. The participants reported that they continued to think about those relationships much more than they noodled over their revealed relationships. In yet another survey of individuals who said they continued to be obsessed with a past relationship, they more often than not reported that it had been a secret one.

So what does all this add up to? Does it mean that while shaving in the morning, you should start practicing your snarl to look mean and lean? Does it mean you should insist the lady keep your relationship a secret? Of course not. It simply means that women love a little mystery, a little secrecy, and a little unpredictability. And they *love* playing seductive games across the restaurant, across the bar, or across the park. And, as soon as you start reading and emitting the signals discussed in *U.S.S.*, not only will you please the lady, but you'll avoid getting turned down when you make the approach.

Why have I spent so much time telling you about phenylethylamine and the excitement/danger aspect of love and about cognitive consistency? Because, once you understand these two concepts, you'll have the power to turn up the heat and get any woman who finds you even moderately attractive incredibly excited over you.

16

The Move That All
Turned-on Women Make

Here's good news: Happily there is one sure-fire, never-fail, always-happens, instantaneous, instinctive move a woman will make whenever she spots a man she likes. Perhaps it comes from childhood when Mom would stick her knuckle in her back and say, "Straighten up, dear. You're so much more attractive that way." After ten, or more, years of connecting good posture with being attractive, it becomes a knee-jerk reaction.

You guys do it too. Often, as I'm walking down to the beach, I'll see a man strolling along the shore on my right, and a woman doing the same in the opposite direction on my left. Their posture is normal, meaning a little slouchy. Perhaps their heads are down searching for seashells, or contemplating the wonder of their navels. But, the moment they spot each other approaching, up comes the shoulders, back goes the head, and their steps become brisker. Once safely past each other, out of eyeshot, they give in again to gravity.

UNDERCOVER SEX SIGNAL #20:

The Perk-up (or Breast Thrust)

Here Ashley, holding her head up by her fist, looks like she's watching a plant grow. Jade is watching the hour-hand creep around her watch. In other words, they are both having a major yawn of a time.

But wait a minute! "What have we here?" Jade says to Ashley. When you walk in the door, Jade perks up and throws her shoulders back. Ashley does the same. Each has not only perked up, but is giving you a double whammy. What other sex signals are they giving you in this picture?

An absence of any of the other signals—like her *not* playing with her jewelry, *not* playing peekaboo, or *not* letting her shoe dangle— does *not* mean she is *not* interested. However, if she does *not* perk up when she sees you, start catching the eye of some other gals and see which percolate and which don't.

17

The Move That Turns
All Women On

As one who shies away from superlatives, I hesitate to say that the following technique using *your* most potent undercover sex signal is sheer sorcery; yet, it is. If the woman in question is at all attracted to you, it will not only get the excitement flowing through her veins (thanks to phenylethylamine) but also cause her to think she is starting to fall in love with you (thanks to cognitive consistency). Let me explain:

Those two grenades right over your nose have the power to detonate a woman's emotions. Just as those with black belts in karate register their fists as lethal weapons, you can register your eyes as psychologically lethal weapons when you master the eye-contact technique which I call "taffy eyes."

I have heard many women say, "I knew he was the one the moment I looked into his eyes." Was it that "he" was so special, or could it be that "he" knew the power of intense eye contact? When you stare deeply into the eyes of a woman (as long as she finds you initially attractive) and keep them there, especially during silences, it works a kind of "magic" on her. Here's proof.

In a study called "The Effects of Mutual Gaze on Feelings of Romantic Love," researchers put 48 men and women who didn't know one another in a big room and assigned them a series of part-ners. Unbeknownst to the subjects, they gave the partners direc-tions on how much eye contact to have with whomever they were speaking. It varied from only 30 percent to more than 70 percent of the time.

Then, afterward, the researchers asked the subjects how they felt about the various people they had spoken with. The results?

> *Subjects who engaged in mutual gaze increased signifi-cantly their feelings of passionate love . . . and liking for their partner.*
>
> Journal of Research in Personality[36]

The Electrifying Power of Eye Contact

Powerful eye contact instantaneously stimulates strong feelings of attachment and affection. Why? Helen Fisher, the aforementioned anthropologist, says that direct eye contact triggers "a primitive part of the human brain, calling forth one of two basic emotions—approach or retreat."[37] In other words, her reaction is one of the most common basic animal instincts, fear—and we now know how that is linked to romance. (Later in *U.S.S.*, you'll see how to use this knowledge for the ideal first date with the lady.)

Look deeply into her eyes, and when you must look away, do so reluc-tantly, slowly, as if pulling your eyes away from hers is as difficult as pulling warm taffy.

Here's where the phenomenon of cognitive consistency comes in. Follow me carefully now: If your slightly exaggerated eye con-tact is giving her that phenylethylamine-filled excitement/fear and you are even moderately attractive to her, she will believe that her own emotions are causing it. Thus, she will begin to actually *feel* the emotion to prove to herself that her mind and body are consistent. (Cognitive consistency, remember?)

Since the little lady's heart will be beating faster and she'll have that tingly feeling all over (unbeknownst to her, just because of your increased eye contact), she will interpret this as the first stages of infatuation with you.

Now, there is a minor risk in using this technique on the street or at work. If the woman is not at all attracted to you, she will interpret your gaze as licentious and lascivious lechery and will dial 911 or get you on a harassment rap. However, and I repeat, *if* she is at all attracted to you, she will see it as your thinking, "Beautiful lady, I can't take my eyes off you." And that, for a woman, is the biggest aphrodisiac of all.

The arguments for intense eye contact are seemingly endless. In addition to lighting her fire, maintaining strong eye contact gives you the impression of being a more intelligent and abstract thinker. Because abstract thinkers integrate incoming data more easily than concrete thinkers do, they can continue looking into someone's eyes even during the silences. Peering into a partner's peepers does not distract their thought processes.[38]

So if the arguments are so overwhelmingly in favor of establishing strong eye contact, why isn't every guy doing it? Because of the big block—especially when it comes to beautiful women. The more someone overwhelms us, the more we avoid their eyes. For example, sometimes the office cleaning staff will avert their gaze from the big boss. And if we meet someone extraordinarily handsome, beautiful, or accomplished we tend to do the same.

Women have an interesting way of expressing feigned shyness and at the same time boldness with their eyes—they flutter them! The longer a woman's lashes, the more she makes use of this maneuver. Fluttering the eyelashes is another of those signals that starts out as an instinctive reaction to internal stimuli. When women become emotional, their eyes tear up and they, of course, must blink to clear them. Recognizing that some men find the eyelash flutter attractive, women affect it.

Do Lasses Like Lads Who Wear Glasses?

With all this talk of intense eye contact, you'd think taking off your glasses would make you more attractive to women. Surprisingly enough, though, that's not the case. A study called "The Effects of Eyeglasses on Perceptions of Interpersonal Attraction," published in the *Journal of Social Behavior and Personality*, found that women like men *better* when they are wearing glasses.[39] (Not so, the other way around.)

The women reported, "It makes a guy look more intelligent. And if the frames are cool, it makes him look super." But beware, gentlemen; your choice of glasses is an important fashion statement; so make sure the frames are up-to-date and are right for your face. If they fit the bill and your beak your glasses are an asset.

18

What Does She Mean When She Says, "You're Just Not My Type"?

When a woman says this, you can interpret it in several ways. But it usually means that pigs will lay eggs before she ever gets in bed with you. So if seduction, not friendship, is your goal, you might as well find another tree to bark up, unless, of course, you want to stick it out until practically every other man in her life is pushing up daisies and you're the last tuna left on the beach.

To be absolutely correct, her saying, "You're just not my type," means, "You don't fit my preexisting and neurophysiological real template of maleness. And, furthermore, all of the neuroemotional development that mediates against the electrochemical activity of certain parts of my brain is insufficient for an intrapsychic event to occur with you."

Now before you feel your family jewels are being pillaged, let's go over what that actually means. Let's say you're better-looking, you make more money, and you're one helluva lot nicer guy than the jerk she's currently seeing.

It doesn't matter. You could be as rich as Bill Gates, as handsome as Tom Cruise, and as nice as Mother Teresa. If you don't fit her love template, you won't score with her. As Johnny Cochran said during the O.J. Simpson trial, "If it doesn't fit, you must acquit." So,

sorry gentlemen, if the little lady says, "You don't fit," you must acquit. After all, she's the world's foremost expert on whom she
wants to sleep with, and whom she doesn't.

A woman's neurons have minds of their own. They tell her
whom she's going to love and whom she's going to sleep with—
often in defiance of anything her logic would recommend. When
you learn to understand her neurobiology and what excites her, it
gives you much more stud status in her eyes than the size of your
biceps, your brain, or any other bodily part she might measure
against your competitor's.

I'm sure you have your preferences too. Some men's "type" is
more general, such as tall blondes or brunette midgets. Millions of
men, however, want something very specific. You need only read
the personals to know that: "SWM seeks a loving relationship with
a one-eyed redhead with big feet." History is fraught with men and
women as kinky as an old phone line. Napoleon is reputed to have
liked his women not kinky but stinky. He once wrote, "My beloved
Josephine, am arriving in Paris tomorrow. Don't wash."

Why am I telling you this? Only to demonstrate how esoteric
taste in love can be. Your choice may be more in the all-vanilla
freezer, but the little lady's may not be. Don't take rejection person-
ally! Just look around and see who craves your flavor.

Why She Digs That Dishpit (and Not Me, F'irnstance)

So why is she turned on by one dude and not another? Why does
one woman push your buttons more than another? Psychology?
Biology? Anthropology? All of the above and a whole lot more.

Actually, Granny had the answer. Whenever I'd express my as-
tonishment that one of my girlfriends had fallen "for such a turkey,"
she'd simply nod her head wisely and say, "Love will go where it's
sent." Did she know she was thus echoing Pascal's wisdom of more
than 300 years ago, "The heart has its reasons, whereof reason

knows nothing"? For those of you who can't trust anyone over 300, that means that "people flip over people for no damn good reason."

Actually, in this case, there is a reason. Mother Nature doesn't just poke the lady one morning, point at you, and say, "Honey, he's the one." Mother Nature doesn't demand that the sound of your voice, the way you laugh, or the way you look at the filly with soulful eyes will make her heart falter, her hands perspire, her feet tingle, and her lips ask you the way to the bedroom. There is a scientifically sound reason why it happens, and I've actually witnessed it in action.

Once, during my modeling years, I was sitting at the bar with my 36C-24-35 roommate enjoying our end-of-the-day munchies, when a very ordinary looking guy—dry brownish hair, medium height, tiny eyes a tad too close together—said with a big grin, "Excuse me, ladies. Do you believe in love at first sight? Or do I have to walk by again?"

Jessica swung her head around, expecting to blow him off as she had done half a dozen others that evening—especially ones with dumb lines like that. This time, however, when Jessica's eyes met his beady little ones, she froze momentarily. Then she turned the revolving stool toward him, tilted her head, and lowered one shoulder. She crossed her legs seductively and said, "You could try."

He shrugged, smiled, and turned to walk back into the crowd. Jessica looked like a locomotive had hit her. Lest he get away and not return, Jessica called after him. "Uh, just kidding," she said.

"I was hoping you'd call me back. Hi, my name is Fausto," he said, extending a hand that Jessica willingly took, "and you must be the lovely Jessica I've heard so much about." He then asked my name, though obviously with less gusto and still holding Jessica's hand.

After a few minutes, I managed to disappear, unnoticed by either, into the crowd. Occasionally, I would glance over at them. Once, Fausto and Jessica were toasting their glasses. Another time,

Jessica was laughing and dusting real or imagined lint off his jacket. The last time I saw them that evening was as they were walking out the door together, perhaps to a music club or perhaps to his apartment—destination unknown.

Later, much later, in the wee hours of the morning, I heard our door open. A giddy Jessica stumbled in, trying to be as quiet as possible, but her hiccups gave her away. I mumbled, "Where have you been?"

"What did you, hic, think of him?" she asked.

"Who, Fabian?" I asked.

"No, silly, hic . . ."

"Flavio?"

"No, Fausto! Isn't he, hic, cool?"

Fortunately, half asleep, I could feign drowsiness to avoid answering.

Jessica and Fausto had a stormy affair for about six months until he finally broke it off. Apparently, she wanted him to commit and he wanted to play the field for a few more years before taking the big step.

Once, in the sad days after they split, I was helping Jessica extract all pictures of Fausto from her photo album. As she turned a page, I said, pointing to a guy standing by an antique car, "Wait, you missed one."

"No, that's my dad when he was younger," she replied. Jessica had always spoken about how much she loved and missed her father and what a close relationship they'd had. But it wasn't until that moment that I knew what he looked like and made the connection between her dad and Fausto. I realized retroactively why Fausto fit Jessica's love mandate.

What Makes Her Feel "in Love" (Romantics, Don't Read This!)

Science, now fully aware that the brain's emotional chemistry can be swayed by, for example, selective seratonin uptake inhibitors like Prozac and Paxil, has discovered that love too can be defined in terms of chemical reactions. You can't make someone love you specifically by giving them a pill, but chemical reactions result from visceral reactions to events and a person's past.

That does not mean that when Jessica spotted beady-eyed little Fausto with his hackneyed pickup line, she thought of her dad. In most cases, in fact, people don't make such a connection. But their incipient feelings of love come from deeply buried responses to sharp cuts of pain or pleasure axed in our brains at an early age. And those responses generate a form of "drug" that circulates through our system.

If you're up for a science moment, read on. If not, skip to the dating mandates below. For those of you whiz kids who are still with me, scientists call this attraction "sexual imprinting." Whatever individual (usually a member of the opposite sex) is around when you are a tot becomes a neural imprint for masculinity or femininity. A sexologist by the name of Dr. John Money coined a more romantic term, "lovemap," for this early imprinting. Whenever we see, feel, hear, or do something that is pleasurable with someone during our tender years, that person's qualities form a menu of what attributes we will flip for later in life. Conversely, early traumatic experiences (which occur daily with 5-year olds) add attributes to the list of "Couldn't possibly go for anybody like that." Money said, "Lovemaps. They're as common as faces, bodies, and brains. Each of us has one. Without it, there would be no falling in love, no mating, and no breeding of the species."[40]

An Austrian scientist, Dr. Konrad Lorenz, once dramatized the significance of the early imprinting phenomenon by snatching a mother duck away just before her little ducks came out of their shells into the cruel world. He then went around the laboratory flapping his wings and quacking. (And we wonder where the term "mad scientist" comes from.) Well, the little ducklings got "imprinted" and began to follow Dr. Lorenz wherever he went.[41]

Very recent research by three psychiatrists, Doctors Thomas Lewis, Fari Amini, and Richard Lannon at the University of California in San Francisco has peeled back yet another layer of what scientists generally accept as the bottom line on love.[42] They were even able to pinpoint the parts of the brain that become sexually imprinted—and they *don't* include the part that controls our reason. The researchers wrote, "The neural systems responsible for emotion and intellect are separate, creating the chasm between them." They're so far apart, in fact, that you'd have to pack a lunch to get from one to the other, thereby explaining why "love is blind."

You can't intellectually choose who is going to charm you any more than you can will yourself to throw a pass like Kurt Warner from the St. Louis Rams. The "requisite neural framework", as the researchers called it, doesn't coalesce on command, and, although you may have seen a terrific "hail Mary pass," you can't direct your body to throw one.

It's the same with love. Like it or not, all of us know only how to play the kind of love games we have already practiced. It made perfect sense that Fausto had pushed Jessica's buttons. She had already practiced loving someone who had looked like him, her dad. In other words, he "fit" the part of her brain that was responsible for love.

So How Can I Make Her Feel That "Chemistry" for Me?

Now, as to the question of "creating chemistry," you can do two things. One is to listen carefully to her while she is speaking and use the same words she does, especially when referring to events and people in her past. If she says, "mother," "mom," "ma," "mummy," or "my old lady,"—you say the same. The second thing you can do is to pay attention to her body language. If she moves in a genteel fashion, you should too. If she's more casual, that should be your style when you're with her. Although to all outward appearances you are different and you think that is the attraction, chemistry "happens" between people who, unbeknownst to even themselves, have a basis of similarity.

Looking for an (Almost) Sure Thing?

Spiritually it's for the birds, but we know that even humans "of a feather" flock together. It sounds contradictory, but it's also true that "opposites attract"—sort of. In love, it's been proven that we only find differences that can enhance our life to be turn-ons. Otherwise, we go for folks just like us.[43]

And here's a fact that really stun-gunned me. It's at least understandable that married couples often resemble each other in age, religion, ethnic background, socioeconomic status, and even political views. But even the researchers were thunderstruck when they discovered that four times higher on the similarity scale were people who had married lookalikes![44] They were similar down to such details as the length of their earlobes, the distances between the eyes, and even the length of their fingers.

When one considers, however, that our "lovemaps" are formed in childhood, it all makes sense. After all, who was around when a woman's sexuality developed? Her father, uncles, brothers, and others who had the same genes. So if you swim after gals who look as though they're in the same gene pool you're in, you're four times as apt to make it with them.

People who were brought up in the same family or even in the same part of the country tend to move like each other. People who think alike tend to move in a similar fashion. And when people are comfortable with us, they subconsciously begin to emulate our movements. If, on the other hand, they don't like us, they purposefully try to move in an opposing way.

UNDERCOVER SEX SIGNAL #21:

The Copycat

When a woman copies your movements, you know she wants to surf on your wavelength. Here Ashley is enjoying listening to Rod and is probably subconsciously copying his motions. Many times when a woman has had an extra drink or two and is feeling very relaxed, she will fall into copying a man's movements—if she likes him. You can even use this as a test. As you lift your glass, see if she lifts hers. Put your elbow on the table and see if she does likewise. (Here's an extra hint: Copy her motions to establish subliminal rapport. She'll start to feel real cozy around you and not know why!) Smart women, especially those trained in NLP or neuro-linguistic programming, often use this "mirroring" effect to establish rapport with someone. But, hey, if she's using it consciously on you, that's cool. It still means she likes you.

Shall I Stick Around for Her to See the Light?

Many men, hopelessly hung up on a particular girl, have asked me, "Even if she's not attracted to me at first, can that change with time? Can she grow to love me?" Very often, a woman will keep a male friend as a security blanket. Usually, she enjoys his being attracted to her but wants to "just be friends." (Ouch!) So the question becomes, "Should I stick around to see if she 'sees the light?'"

Since no two people are alike, no two answers to that can be alike. But here are some guidelines (first the bad news for lovelorn men and then the semi-good news). If you feel that she is one of those women who habitually gets themselves into destructive relationships for some deep-seated psychological reason as we discussed earlier, or that she is untrustworthy, then the answer is no. You, as a nice guy, should probably split, because even if she did commit to you there would be tremendous problems afterward.

If she's a principled person, however, and her other relationship doesn't work out, she might feel "her biological clock ticking." Or she might even consciously tell herself that, because you are such a good guy, she can grow to love you. And she probably will!

You may have noticed above that I said "*semi*-good news." The reason is because she will most likely never love you in that hot passionate dying to jump your bones every minute type of lustful love that might cross your mind (like all the time). Quite a few of my girlfriends have wound up loving and marrying a forever-faithful male friend. So if having a woman's love but not her lust is enough for you, hang in there. (But cover your bets by letting her know that you're dating other people too!)

Undercover Sex Signals Are Nothing New

I recently told my grandmother I was writing this book and asked her if women were as aggressive when she was young. Her response was just a smile.

"Did you make the first move with Grandpa?" I asked.

Now her smile turned to a sweet mixture of coyness and nostalgia, which for an 86-year-old woman is pretty good. I could tell there were a few sexy skeletons in her closet.

"Really, Granny, if you were interested in a man, how would you let him know?"

Her wrinkled fingers began caressing her crepelike neck, and a far-away look came into her faded eyes. "Oh, we had our little ways."

I'll bet she did! At that moment, with her tiny smile and tilted head, the decades tumbled away, and Granny looked very beautiful, almost sensual to me. And then she added, "But Grandpa never knew it."

I'm grateful to Granny that she gave such good undercover sex signals; otherwise, I wouldn't be here to clue you in on what's happening all around you.

Using U.S.S.s to Succeed with Women

19

You Never Have to Hear "No" Again

So far, we've discussed the power and the prevalence of undercover sex signals and why spotting them is like trying to find a goose in a snowstorm for many men. We've proven how incredibly aggressive women are in wanting to meet you, and why they feel like brides left at the altar when you don't acknowledge their unspoken overtures. Now is the time to talk about solving both those problems with just a little consciousness raising.

The first man I ever met who was consciously aware of undercover sex signals was my dentist, Daniel. (Yes my *dentist*! I spoke briefly about him earlier.) Dr. Dan bears a striking resemblance to a bleached seal—with a pointy face and a laughable moustache—yet he never leaves a party or bar without a smiling girl on his flipper. In fact, he has such a rich history of success with women that his friends say that as an infant he grabbed for the nurse instead of the bottle. But Daniel thoroughly enjoys his triumphs. In fact his motto is "Life, liberty, and the happiness of pursuit."

I found out about his conquests some years ago while waiting for a dental appointment. I was chatting with his receptionist, telling her about my book on love and she said, "Oh, you should talk to Dr. Dan. He's quite a lady-killer."

"Really?" I responded thinking, "You've got to be kidding!" She continued, "Dr. Daniel never ever goes to a function—a chamber of commerce event, a dental convention, a party, a fund-raiser, a wedding, or even a funeral without leaving with one of the attractive unattached women there." With a touch of awe, she said, "Other men are totally bewildered." As though reading my mind, she added an afterthought, "Actually, I am too."

The Man Who Looked Like a Seal, and Scored Like a Stallion

I started picturing Dr. Daniel's being suave with women. It was a bit difficult to conjecture, as he is a little pudgy, about 5'10", and wears his graying hair combed straight back, which, unfortunately, only enhances his seal-like appearance. Even a generous appraiser wouldn't bestow him more than a 4.5 on a scale of 10.

When it came time for my appointment, I leaned back and, as usual, opened my mouth in the obligatory "Ahh" position. As he dove in with his pick and mirror to inspect my aching third left molar, he asked, "So, Leil, what's the title of your new book?"

I garbled, "Hah er Ake Huhuhundy Hall Ng Uv Ith Uh."

"Really?" Daniel said. "*How to Make Anybody Fall in Love With You.* That sounds interesting. Where are you getting your information?"

"Huhis and ersoul huherhie."

"Oh, studies and personal interviews. Hey, you should interview me," he said, "I have quite an active dating life." At that moment, I thought of two unsolved mysteries in my life. One is how dentists can translate patients' stretched-mouth garbling into English; the other is how Dr. Daniel, the human turnip, could be popular with women. He said if I'd have dinner with him, he would share his secrets with me.

"Hur, Uid hur fo." He understood, correctly, that I meant, "Sure,

I'd love to." Since, as the receptionist had told me, Dan's reputation of being an extremely successful womanizer has spread far and wide, that was an offer I couldn't refuse.

As the evening of our interview approached, I wrote down all the questions I wanted to ask him, such as "How do you first get the woman to notice you?" and "What is your first move?" It continued through "How do you ask her out?" and culminated with "Do you have any special techniques to bed her?"

It was arranged that he would ring my bell, I'd come down, and we'd walk over to O'Neals, a chic and popular SoHo bar/restaurant where a lot of beautiful single people in Manhattan hang out (and where, incidentally, the photos in this book were shot). When we arrived, the bar section looked like the backstage area at the "Miss America" pageant. There were loads of women and men eyeing each other, each hoping to pair off with an exciting new stranger for dinner and who knows what else.

As we entered, Daniel's eyes surveyed the room with the care of an airline pilot examining the horizon to avoid a midair crash. We managed to sidle up to the bar and found two just-deserted stools that a couple heading for the dining room had vacated.

"So, do you see anyone you like?" I asked.

"If I may correct you," he said gently, "that's not the right question, Leil. You should ask, 'Do I see any women who like me?' "

"Excuse me?"

"I'll let you in on a little secret but only if you promise not to tell the girls in my office. They call me 'Romeo' or 'Don Juan,' and they think I can 'get' any woman I want. That's not exactly the way it is," he said with a smiling touch of self-deprecation. "I can pretty well rope in any woman who wants to meet me though."

"Well, how do you know who wants to meet you?" I asked.

"Well, for example, there are, oh, about 30 women at the bar, wouldn't you say?"

"Yes," I replied.

"There are three or four who for sure want to meet me and another half-dozen I could approach and probably get. Let's start with the three who I know are shoe-ins. First, there's the brunette who's thrown three or four sideways glances my way. Then there's the redhead who ran her hands through her hair and smiled at me. Whew, then there's that knockout brunette who just took off her glasses when I looked her way."

"Her mother probably told her 'Men seldom make passes at girls who wear glasses,'" I suggested.

"Not true," Dan said, "I'd make a dive for her if she were wearing SCUBA goggles. Ah ha! That clinches it. She put the tip in her mouth. She's hot!"

He continued, "Those are the only three women in the room that I'm *sure* of success with. Which one would you like me to meet?"

"OK," I challenged him, "try the hot one."

"Fine," he said. "By the way, what town were you born in?"

"Me? Uh, Bethesda, Maryland."

"OK," he said, "you're my cousin visiting from Bethesda."

Daniel disappeared into the throng and five minutes later returned, gracefully cutting a path through the crowd for Ms. Swizzle Stick, who was, sure enough, following him like a cocker-spaniel pup follows its parent.

"Lydia," he said to her, "this is my cousin Leil. She thought that what you were drinking looked good and wanted to ask what it was and how you make it. I can drink, but I'm a lousy bartender," he said with a smile. "Perhaps you two women can share recipes, if that doesn't sound too sexist."

"Ooh, Danny, it's a Ruby Fizz, and I'll bet you're not as bad a bartender as you think you are. Why don't you guess what's in it?" she asked, lifting the drink and her straw to his lips.

"Boy, he's really pushed her buttons," I thought. And so he had. The two of them chatted few minutes more, they exchanged phone numbers, and he vowed to call.

I complimented Dr. Dan on his successful pursuit.

"Leil," he replied, "*she* was doing the pursuing. I was merely letting her be successful. You know, reading a woman's ready signals isn't rocket science."

UNDERCOVER SEX SIGNAL #22:

The Suggestive Suck

It doesn't take a biology degree to understand the significance of a woman's putting something in her mouth when she is excited over a man. Often, a woman will combine one of the other signals, such as *The Shoe Dangle* or *The Eyelash Flutter*, with sucking on a swizzle stick, plastic spoon, or even the tip of her finger, as Ashley was doing in *The Exposé* sex signal. Here Tanya is letting a swizzle stick work its magic on the man.

"No, it's tougher than rocket science for most men," I replied. "It's like reading a road map is for women."

With certain other mammals, it's easy to see when they are turned on. In some species, the skin around the female's vagina changes color when the female is in heat. The female guinea pig's vagina actually closes up when the animal is currently not available.[45] (You may have seen women with that expression on their faces.)

However, even fully clothed, a woman's body language is just as obvious when she spots a man she likes. In fact, a turned-on woman is as evident as a 747 in a cornfield to a guy like Dan. His philosophy is plain and simple. *Why bark up wrong trees and risk rejection? Climb up a sure thing and pick all the fruit you want.*

Meanwhile, Back at the Bar

Dr. Dan and I took a table in the restaurant section of O'Neals, where we could get a good view of everyone coming in the door and of the crowd at the bar. Each person who entered the bar got a thinly disguised once-over from practically everyone who was not dining.

We had been watching for about 10 minutes when a man who could have played the part of a young John Wayne sauntered in. It was as though the handsome actor in full cowboy regalia had kicked open the saloon door. I didn't know which woman to watch first. Most of the women at the bar had visceral reactions. Several who were facing the door on stools uncrossed their legs. The ones who were standing straightened up, as they tucked in their tummies and thrust out their breasts. One kept her eyes on him and ran her hand through her hair.

The cowboy walked briskly up to the bar, slammed a few dollars down, and must have said "Gimme a beer." Rudely rejecting the glass the bartender offered, he grabbed the bottle and, turning around to face the gathering, put both elbows back on the bar in a tough "I'm the bouncer in the devil's saloon" stance. When he faced toward us, we could see his cocky twisted smile and his razor-pointed snakeskin boots that could kill a mosquito in the corner.

This obviously didn't fly with most of the women, who went back to their conversations with girlfriends.

For a few others, his "I use barbed wire for dental floss" look was still a turn-on. The drama unfolding before my eyes was riveting. As he drank his beer from the bottle, I looked around the bar. One woman who obviously had not been turned off by his lethal leathery appearance pushed her hair over one eye and started pulling a string on her dress. (See Jade in *The Jewelry Tug*.) Another moistened her lips with her tongue, gave him a sly smile, and then looked down. (See Sandy in *The Lips Lick*.)

Apparently, that was the one he fancied—and he smiled back. Right on cue, as Dan predicted, she looked down. Dan said, "OK, Leil, set your stopwatch. She's going to look up again in less than a minute."

And 15 seconds later, indeed she did. The cowboy gave her an asymmetrical sarcastic smile that seemed to please his target lady. She smiled back at him, and he sauntered over to her.

Why are women's reactions to the cowboy significant in our discussion of U.S.S.s? Because the way a man comports himself in those first minutes is far more important to a woman than the other way around. Let's say you spot a walking centerfold, a "10," a real traffic stopper. Almost nothing she could do would gross you out. You'd still let her eat crackers in your bed.

Not so with women. From the moment they spot you, you are on trial—because a female has a very different mechanism working in her brain than you have working in yours (surprise, surprise). You can get sexually turned on by a woman you might never want a relationship with—the gorgeous gun moll, the knockout with bust size 38 and an IQ to match, the hooker who dresses up like Minnie Mouse—all lovely company for one night, maybe two nights if she's lucky, but definitely not the type you'd want to raise a family with.

Women, generally, look at sex a different way. Although the new liberated woman doesn't have to be in love with you to want a roll in the hay, she needs to "feel something" for you. It's all part of Mother Nature's plan.

Throughout the animal kingdom, the male can mate with many females and not be hung up during the gestation period and beyond. But in all mammals, the female must bear the offspring.

She is, in a sense, also responsible for keeping up the quality of the species. For that reason, she is going to be far more affected by her neural imprinting, the concept of being attracted to family look-alikes, than you. Evolutionary theorists tell us that, even when considering one-night nookie with a nerd she never wants to see again, a woman subconsciously listens to her genes.

"So How Do I Appeal to Her, uh, Neural Imprinting?"

Well, for starters, either you do or you don't. But even if you don't, all is not lost. No matter what features Mother Nature gave you, there are lots of things you can do to tip the scale in your favor. Men are continually asking in my class, "Do women like it if I . . . do this? or that? or the other." Unfortunately, my answer always has to be the same. It depends on the woman. No one style pleases all.

Dealing with women makes a man feel like a termite in a yo-yo. You're one dame's dream man and another's nightmare. One babe thinks you're big bucks; another says, "You're flat broke." To impress one woman, you have to win the Nobel Peace Prize; for another, just keep your nose clean and stay out of the slammer.

There are, of course, a few generalizations. For example, she probably doesn't like for you to pass gas in public, force her to listen to your interminable series of long monologues about how magnificent you are, take her to an expensive restaurant and discover you forgot your wallet, or paint yourself as a needy little twerp by

laying out a pathetic personal life. But, aside from those few generalizations, one size does not fit all.

> Whether the woman who digs you owns controlling interest in all of cre-
> ation or has cobwebs in her wallet, she sends you subtle signals across the
> bar, across the men's-socks counter at Macys, and across the baseball sta-
> dium. Now the ball's in your court.

Sure, make a pass at the ones you like. But if you never want to
face rejection again, throw your pass at one who sends the right
signals.

I will, of course, give you the results of my findings as to what
the *majority* of women like, so you can amplify your opportunity
in any situation. These will be interspersed between the undercover sex signals.

The main message here is to get hep to her undercover sex signals. John F. Kennedy's words will ring throughout the ages: "Ask
not 'What can my country do for me?' Ask 'What can I do for my
country?'"

Well, the motto for the man who is always successful with
women, the U.S.S. Man, is "Ask not 'Who most turns me on?' Ask
'Who am I most turning on?'" Then, pick the juiciest peach from
that tree. You know you will at least agree with her on one thing:
she has excellent taste in men!

Run Yourself up the Flagpole
(and See Which Skirts Salute)

Any guy with the brains to pull his head in before closing the window knows that one has to do a little market research before rolling

out a product. Unfortunately, many men forget this principle of business when it comes to selling themselves to women.

Dan told me about a friend of his who taught him the importance of doing a little market research as far as people are concerned. He had a roommate named Hardeep when they were both just getting started in dentistry. Hardeep was a handsome, tall, fairly dark-skinned second-generation Indian chap with bushy eyebrows and a big smile. They rented a nice apartment overlooking the water in Huntington, Long Island, a fairly homogeneous upper-middle-class suburb of New York. Practically every weekend, the two friends would go to Huntington clubs, bars, dances, and discos together, both hoping to meet women. But poor Hardeep was batting zero with the women of Huntington.

At about this time, young Dan was just getting hep to the body-language thing and was starting to be successful with women. Most nights he'd leave the club with one of the local beauties on his arm, but poor Hardeep always went home alone.

On a hunch, Dan suggested that the next weekend they go to a club in New York City where singles went to do Latin dancing.

"But I don't know how to do any Latin dances," protested Hardeep.

"Don't worry about it," Dan told him. The following Friday, Dan and Hardeep walked into a hip Latino club in Manhattan. Poor Aryan-looking Dan wasn't getting much of an eye from the Latin lovelies. But Hardeep was making a lot of women touch their necks, lick their lips, caress their arms, etc. It didn't matter that he didn't know how to do the Latin dances. Within 10 minutes, Hardeep had a stunning teacher only too willing to show him the steps—and a lot more if he wanted it. And that night it was Dan who went home alone.

Dan and Hardeep remained friends and roommates but didn't go to the same clubs anymore. Hardeep found that white middle-class girls didn't go for him as much as did women in some of the hipper clubs around Manhattan. He became a regular at those spots and, according to Dan, can now do a pretty impressive tango and merengue.

If the fish aren't biting, you don't necessarily have to change the bait. Try a new stream. And if the babes aren't biting there, try playing in a new neighborhood. (If they're *still* not biting, it's time to take a good look at the bait.)

20

How to Become a Sexual Polygraph Machine

Let's say you walk into a room and your eyeballs start whirling like a propeller on a beanie cap at the knockout standing by the buffet table. She turns her head, takes one look at you, and it's already happened. It's over. Like a horse at an auction, you have been officially appraised; she has decided on the spot whether you are a top-grade champion, or a nag to be sold to the glue factory. Women are absolutely ruthless in their snap judgments about men. They're also very susceptible to what their girlfriends think. That's why you often see them talking to each other, whispering while looking at you.

Generally, a woman puts a man into one of four categories:

> **A Winner:** She thinks, *"Ooh, he is so cool!"* She wants you! And unless you do something really dumb to screw up, it's a sure thing.

> **A Possible:** She thinks, *"Hmm, not bad."* But the jury is still out on you. Be on your toes.

> **A Loser:** She thinks, *"I hope he doesn't try to hit on me."* You have got to be pretty swift to turn this one around.

A F.U.C.: (A Funny Undesirable Creep). She thinks, "*Yuuuuch!*" Give up.

You may rightfully ask, "Once she's sized me up on looks alone, can I get reclassified once we've met?" Sure, there is indeed some migration among the four classes. *A Possible* can become *A Winner* if he plays his cards right. He can also slip to being *A Loser* with one dumb move. *A Loser* can even work his way up to being *A Winner* over time. There are also combos, such as *Possible/Winner* and *Possible/Loser*. However the last category, *A Funny Undesirable Creep* is different; once a *F.U.C.* almost always a *F.U.C.*

But the most important concept to grasp here is that one woman's *Winner* is another woman's *Loser* and vice versa, with all the variations. Assuming you're not a total *F.U.C.* (if you were, you wouldn't have had the sense to buy this book), let's get to work.

A full 99.99 percent of men look around a group and ask themselves, "Which of the women here do I like?" Most guys walk into a party like a penis with a man attached. Their peter meters point at the most attractive woman in the room, and they spend the rest of the evening conniving to meet her, jumping though hoops trying to entertain her, and finally, as she leaves with some other guy, feeling like failures. Meanwhile, there are a half-dozen or so sexy ladies who have been throwing sex signals at them like rice at a wedding. And they've been missing every kernel. Your *first* question, instead, should be, "Which of these women likes me?" Then your *second* should be, "Of these women who like me, which ones do I like?"

Remember Dr. Dan's prescription for sure success.

Ask Ye Not, "Who Turns Me On?"
Ask, Rather, "Who Do I Turn On?"

Force your eyes to scan every room you walk into. Whether you're in the Metropolitan Museum of Art in New York City, on Malibu Beach in California, or in a sports bar in Humboldt, Kansas, the signals are all the same. The wealthy heiress with the classy chassy, the *Baywatch* beach babe, and the blitzed blonde bombshell make essentially the same moves. How do we know this? Dozens of studies have confirmed it.

To cite just one, there was a German scientist, Dr. Abel, who specialized in ethology, the study of characteristic behavior patterns in a species. In the 1960s he traveled to various parts of the world with a secret angular lens to photograph strangers trying, successfully and unsuccessfully, to pick each other up. He took his clandestine crooked camera to sophisticated occidental countries like France and oriental spots like Japan. He also photographed couples getting to know each other in more primitive parts of the globe, such as Samoa, Amazona, and Papua New Guinea.[46]

He then analyzed all the flirting sequences and discovered that whether the female was born with a silver spoon in her mouth or a bone ring in her nose, women around the globe flirt with the same signals and often in the same sequence. And they often start in the same way little girls do, with an attention-getting device like making a noise, giggling, or raising their arms. The more sophisticated ladies, whether they were in the jungle on the outskirts of Monrovia or in the single's zoo in midtown Manhattan, found caressing or exposing parts of the body to be quite effective.

21

From Meeting to Mating, Easy Does It

Gentlemen, lest some of you feel you've been lax in neglecting to make passes at the lasses you've lusted for, relax. You see, you probably think that dame hunting is *your* responsibility every time you walk into a social jungle. Think again. Females luring males for the purpose of mating is part of nature's grandiose design. In the animal kingdom, females attract males by hooting, crowing, scratching, stomping, hopping, darting, wiggling, and a myriad of other sex signals. Human women do the same. Nature embedded sex signals in *all* females to propagate the species.

Take rats, for instance, and we've all known a few of those. But let's talk about the hairy four-legged ones that you find under that sink you haven't cleaned in a couple of years. The same researcher who conducted the famous studies that elevated the status of "the pickup" to thesis-worthy material, Dr. Timothy Perper, spied on a rat's pad to document their hanky panky.

First, the female rat sniffs the male rat, and, if she likes his, um, cologne, she faces him and gazes into his baby blacks for a few extra seconds. Then she stiffens her legs and does what is called a "hop and dart." Naturally, she stops just long enough for the male, who is now chasing her, to catch and mount her. Then the games begin. She shakes the rat off and does another "hop and dart." This goes on for as long as *she* decides until he is finally permitted "penile intromission," but no ejaculation. However, if the rat-stud has done well in playing the "hop and dart" game, she does eventually permit ejaculation as well.[47] (Are you beginning to see why I'm telling you this?)

Now, all of this chasing, mounting, shaking, stopping, hopping, and darting may look the same to the untrained observer. But the discriminating eagle-eyed Dr. Perper saw tremendous differences in his rats. Sometimes, the total series took only two minutes. At other times, it took 10 attempts for the dude rat to score. Sometimes, the happy couple would stay together afterward and copulate again. At other times, the male would race outta there like a rat out of hell. But the bottom line is this: The cool male rat that knew how to play the hop and dart game got laid the most. (Now, for sure, you see the parallel.)

That brings us to the subject at hand. Dr. Perper, having gotten the hang of watching horny mammals while conducting such experiments, decided to graduate to horny homo sapiens. He wanted to see if there was a pattern to pickups, both successful and unsuccessful. So, peering over a newspaper while at a singles bar, he spied on couples getting to know each other. He took careful note of who cast the initial glance and how. He recorded who made the initial move and how, who lost interest and why, and who left together and why.

Night after night, the good doctor stayed tirelessly in his smoke-filled laboratory, scribbling notations, devising charts, and hypothesizing formulas, as men and women picked each other up. Repeatedly, he saw the same pattern of success and the same pattern of failure. Then, in the finest scientific tradition, he broke the body-language pattern of couples who *succeeded* in getting to know each other into very specific steps.

Often, Dr. Perper observed, the woman would cast a signal but the male would not respond appropriately. And she would thus lose interest and start her courtship game with another male.

The steps you must follow after the woman gives you a U.S.S. are as clear and as carefully choreographed as a simple fox trot. But if you slip on any of them, your relationship will veer off the runway, crash, and burn before it ever achieves altitude. If you memorize the following steps, you'll always take off with the lady.

Unfortunately, for being so "evolved," many male humans didn't turn out to be even as smart as rats in picking up on a female's sex signals. So here's "The Pickup Polka," step-by-step.

SECTION V

"The Perfect Pickup"
(in 5 Easy Steps)

22

The Perfect Pickup
Is a Science

Dr. Perper proved, beyond any reasonable doubt, that there are precise steps for the "dance" that must take place if a male/female relationship is going to happen. Women know the steps to this dance by heart, because, long before they were old enough to practice it, they were dreaming of it. When you and your buddies were drawing pictures of navy jets and, pencil in hand, making those funny guy noises, "Rrrrrch, crash! ruum ruum," we girls were making up love stories for our dolls. Barbie meets Ken and all that.

You walk into a club and BLAM; your eyeballs do a slam dunk right into a beautiful blonde sitting at the bar. When she sees you, she begins to run her fingers across her upper chest. You try to put your eyeballs back in their sockets. She casts you a small, almost imperceptible, smile. *Remember that you MUST return her smile; if you don't she will give up and move on to* another guy. But no leering grin here. Match her smile precisely. Be cool.

So far, you've done great. You smiled at her, and when she sneaked another peek at you, you smiled again, and maybe even gave her a little nod.

The Sparks Fly When the Energy Matches

It is crucial to keep the intensity of your smile at about the same level as hers. She smiles a tiny half-smile? You do the same. She gives you a big grin? You do the same. She speaks energetically? You do the same. Research has proven that if your intensity level is much higher or much lower than the woman's, the relationship aborts before it ever gets on the runway. In fact, this is so important that I often call this verbal signal the 27th undercover sex signal. Studies show that a simple verbal missmatch can fizzle a fire before it ever gets lit.

There are many dozens of sex signals that a woman uses to lure a potential partner, and the important thing is, whichever one she casts your way, you MUST always give the appropriate response within the context of the following five steps.

23

How to Make the Approach

We have talked about acknowledging her signal and responding with the same intensity and a touch of playfulness. Let us now move on to making the approach.

A U.S.S.-savvy man never "sneaks up" on a woman from behind. You should wait until she catches your eye. When she does, you must approach her slowly so she can see you coming. Always try to approach a woman head-on so she can see your full body. (When approaching a man, on the other hand, a head-on approach should be avoided. He could interpret it as threatening.)

You might indicate the chair or stool next to her and ask, "May I?" You then sit down and *face in the same direction the lady is facing*. Make sure your body stays at a respectful distance away from her but close enough to allow easy conversation. The noise level of the room, its size, and other variables will dictate the "correct" distance.

If you are alongside of her, start by just looking ahead. If she is attracted to you, this will tantalize her. She'll wonder why you aren't coming on to her, and she may be the one to speak first. Also, be careful that you do not come within her personal space as you are sitting down or getting up on to the stool.

Starting Position to the Perfect Pickup: Strategic Placement

Once you have determined that she has given you one or more of the undercover sex signals, you should approach. You can either stand or be seated next to the lady, but do NOT face her yet. Let her have time to notice that you are there and to size you up before you speak to her.

Do You Pass Muster, Mister?

Gentlemen, remember, during those first few moments when you're meeting a woman, she is analyzing, critiquing, judging, and noodling over your every move, so you have to be on your toes and not miss a trick.

Once, when I was in a college play, my drama teacher, ready to tear his hair out (although he would have preferred tearing mine out) because of my bad acting, shouted, "No, your body is belying your words. Every tiny movement, every body position," he howled, "divulges your private thoughts. Your face can make seven thousand different expressions, and each exposes precisely who you are and what you are thinking." Then he said something I'll never forget: "And your body! The way you move is your autobiography in motion."

How right he was! On the stage of real life, whether you're in front of an audience of a thousand or walking from the bar to the men's room, every physical move you make subliminally tells every woman in the bar the story of your life. (Well, that's a slight exaggeration, but they definitely form an opinion of you just from the way you move.)

Just as dogs hear sounds that our ears can't detect and bats see shapes in the darkness that elude our eyes, females pick up moves that are beneath a male's consciousness. And those moves can result in either a "go" or a "no-go" decision. Every step, every smile, every frown, and every burp that comes out of your mouth can be crucial. A woman gets a "feeling" about you. It's what she calls "women's intuition." She either likes you or she doesn't. On a conscious level, she may not be aware of why. But from just a few moments of watching you in action, she knows whether you have a chance with her or not.

Think of being with her in a complex box wired with circuits to record all the signals flowing between the two of you. She'll pick up as many as 10,000 units of information about you every second.[48] With the zillions of subtle actions and reactions zapping back and forth and forming her opinion, you're going to have to be as careful as a fry cook in a nudist colony.

If you're not quite sure of your movements, turn on the television during any time of day that men are supposedly not watching. Take careful note of the first little girl's or grown up girl's hero you see. If you've chosen to do your research on Saturday morning, you'll see the cartoon characters little girls swoon over. See how the handsome prince or determined avenger walks and talks. Conducting your investigation weekdays, you'll see the soap-opera characters big girls swoon over. See how the handsome husband or determined lover walks and talks.

Kissing a Woman the Way She Likes to Be Kissed

Oh, and incidentally, gentlemen, while you've got the shows on, take note of how the heroes kiss. Girls tell each other if you're a lousy kisser or a great kisser. In fact, an important factor when a girl considers whether or not to sleep with you will be how you kiss. I kid you not!

The TV heroes do it right, fellas: cupping the lady's face in his hands, gently touching her cheek, outlining her lips with his finger, and scooping her up in his arms. You'll probably split your sides laughing at the way the males in the soap operas express passion, but she won't!

Back to our dame chase.

The Game Begins in Earnest

Now, the game begins in earnest. At this point, you are seated next to Ashley and, since you do not know her, you must think of a "natural and neutral" thing to say to her. The best opening phrase (notice I did *not* say "line") is something complimentary and neutral.

Step One to the Perfect Pickup:
The Head Turn

Once you have determined she has given you one or more of the undercover sex signals, you should find something neutral to say to her—
perhaps a light compliment on a piece of jewelry. That is merely an excuse
to turn your head toward her to begin the communication process.
Remember, your body language is far more important than your words. At
this point, only turn your head when speaking with her...so as not to
come on too strong.

You notice that Ashley is wearing a pretty string of pearls. You turn your head toward her and compliment her on them. Ashley, also turning her head, says, "Thank you, they were a gift from my sister who lives in Hawaii."

"Oh, really?" you say, now feigning great interest in anyone living in Hawaii.

Your comment is, of course, just an excuse to get to first base, which is turning just your head toward her. Turning your torso or knees this early would be coming on too strong.

"It must be nice to have a sister living there," you say. You notice she lights up at the mention of Hawaii, so you keep that subject going.

Continue speaking with her with only your head turning toward her unless, of course, she escalates the encounter—as Ashley did. If she does, you, of course, follow suit. You are playing her game well, so keep speaking in more or less the same position until she seems to thaw out even more. At that point, she should start to pivot her body toward you. You should follow suit.

Step Two to the Perfect Pickup: The Torso Turn

Now is the time to gradually let your upper body pivot toward her. If the woman you are speaking with likes you, she will instinctively do the same. Ideally, she will initiate the face-to-face position and you can counter each of her pivots with your own toward her. If she is not showing obvious signs of a meltdown, be on the lookout for some of the other signals we've discussed. Is she running her hand through her hair?

Is she putting a swizzle stick in her mouth? Is she pulling her dress aside to expose more skin? If the answer to any or all of those questions is yes, and if, as a result you decide that she likes you, you can initiate step 3. Start to turn more toward her, but proceed cautiously.

> In the Bible, judgment day comes last. With babes, it comes first. The initial conversation you have with her determines whether you might possibly be part of her past and present someday.

Your first words should always be neutral, courteous and not too private. If you are talking to her at a party, ask her how she knows the host. If it's at an entertainment event, ask her how she is enjoying it. Just make sure your questions are not ones that can be answered by a simple "yes" or "no." Ask open-ended questions to get her talking. When she is speaking, take careful note of her body language. When she seems pleased, stay on that subject. If she starts to turn away or her eyes "glaze over," get off that horse. Your moves are not flying.

It's during this initial conversation that a woman decides whether you're boyfriend material or not, so you want to discuss the subject that is most interesting to her—her! Get her talking about herself.

> The way to make a big hit with a chick is be the (rare) guy who gets her to talk about herself. Where did she grow up? What was her childhood like? Does she like her job? Yada, yada, yada.

A good gambit is to get a "baby-names" book. (You heard right.) Then tell her what her name means. For example "Darlene" means "little darling" in French, "Doris" is Greek for "from the sea," "Amy" is Latin for "beloved," and all forms of "Susie" or "Susan" are Hebrew for "rose." You're safe unless she happens to be named, say, "Debbie," which means "meddlesome bee."

Mesmerize Her with Your Voice

Your initial conversation is also the time to take extra care with something you may never have thought of before—your voice. Whenever you meet a woman, an entire 50 percent of her first opinion of you is determined by how you look. Another whopping 30 percent is determined by how you sound; this has little to do with *what* you say; what you say is not as important as *how* you say it.

Incidentally, women are far more sensitive to the sound of one's voice than you are. Unless a woman sounds like she's hog calling, you probably won't take special note of her voice. Women listen to the tone, the timbre, and the speed with which you speak.

A woman wants to hear a resonant low voice with a little variety to make it interesting. Also, slow down. Most men speak too quickly, especially when they're nervous. Slower speech makes you appear stronger and more confident. She'll feel more relaxed with you. If you do a little work on it ahead of time so it sounds natural, you can mesmerize a woman with your voice alone.

What kind of voice turns women on? One study, called "Voice and Interpersonal Attraction," said that women prefer a voice that is "bright" and capable of a variety of inflections but is of low timbre and without a large range of vocal pitch. In other words, one that is expressive but not all over the field.[49]

Many women will give up on you and not beckon twice if you don't pick up on their first signal. *Look around the minute you walk in* and reward each woman who signals you by flashing her with a smile. That's "reserving" your spot with her so she doesn't try another guy. Then make your choice and approach.

Now, don't go around trying to sound like a DJ. If you do and you're caught by surprise—say the bartender knocks a drink over in your lap—and you yelp two octaves higher than you've been speaking, she won't be very impressed. Speak to her in good low normal tones (and don't cup your hand over your ear like a rock star in rehearsal when you do).

Let's say that, luckily, Ashley, the girl you've been trying to impress digs your act. Your conversation is making beautiful music together, so keep on going. If she seems to get turned off by any subject, get off it fast! You don't want your theme to be the swan song.

"Hawaii is the one place I've always wanted to go," you lie. "Tell me about it." Cool, you noticed she was getting a little bored with the current subject but seemed more lively when talking about the Big Island. So you brought the subject back to Hawaii, you devil you. (That's a good U.S.S. move we'll discuss in more detail when we get to the verbal part of your pickup. Right now, we're concentrating primarily on crucial body language.)

At the end of another 15 minutes or so of conversation, you are both smiling and laughing and your bodies have gradually swiveled toward each other. So far, so great. You're on the mark and headed straight for Ashley's boudoir.

Step Three to the Perfect Pickup: The Body Turn

Now is the time to let your body gradually turn fully toward hers. *Gradually!* It's better if she takes the lead and you follow suit. But if she doesn't, you may move in that direction. Then wait for her to follow *before* turning a little more toward her. Too fast? You lose.

While talking, get on a double track. In addition to thinking about what you're saying, keep your eyes tuned for how she's reacting. Is she smiling a lot? Are her eyes sparkling? Is she leaning in toward you? Or does she look like she'd rather be picking dead flies off flypaper than talking with you?

Fortunately, you've executed your every move with finesse. You never moved to face her any more than was reciprocated by her. For instance, after you had turned your torso toward her you waited for her to turn hers before starting to turn your knees toward her. Good.

At this point, if she thinks you're not too shabby, she may even reach out and touch you. That's hot, and you must show her you enjoy it by perhaps moving into her touch ever so slightly. Maybe she gives you a slight brush of her hand while passing you some peanuts. Or she picks a piece of lint off your jacket. Do not, with your analytical, problem-solving-type guy brain even consider it has anything to do with the lint on your sweater. That would make you stiffen up, and she, being the expert in sex signals that she is, would interpret that as pulling back. If she touches you in any way, that's a sizzler, and you must show how much you enjoy it.

By now, you and a very turned-on flirtatious Ashley are leaning slightly toward each other to close the distance between you. Everything's going great. But watch out. Here's where you start to screw up.

At one point when you leaned a little closer, you forgot to wait for Ashley to do the same. So you leaned in even a little more. Ashley pulls back just a tiny millimeter. You, unaware of her microscopic recoiling, stand your ground. (You should have pulled back a tad at this point and waited for her to move in.) Ashley excuses herself to go to the ladies room. You sense her mysterious coldness and wrack your brain for what you could have said wrong.

It's a common mistake. Most guys, being totally spaced out and glassy-eyed when it comes to body language, think it's something they *said*. Nine times out of ten, it has nothing to do with words.

Happily, however, Ashley returns and seems as friendly as ever, and once again the two of you are in animated conversation, facing each other. At one point, Ashley sees a long brown hair on your jacket and reaches over to pull it off. Teasingly she asks, "Oh, do you prefer brunettes?"

"Damn," you think to yourself. "I knew I should have gotten that jacket cleaned after the big date with Diana last week." However, you catch yourself and come up with a great response. With a big smile you say, "Not now!" But it's too late. Your momentary embarrassment and displeasure had made your body recoil slightly.

Ashley misinterprets your sinking back as a retreat, which hurts her pride, and she too retreats. Oops, you let a moment of awkward silence go down. *Fill the silence, remember?*

But, alas, you don't.

"Well," she chirps up, "it's been great talking with you. I see an old friend over there." Ashley dismounts from the stool and, swinging her hips, walks close to the good-looking guy who's been leaning against the wall, thumbs in pockets, and smiling at her.

"Uh, yeah, see you around." You lose. She loses. It's a lose-lose situation and all because you weren't hep to U.S.S.s.

Later, much later, that night, staring into your empty fridge, you can't figure where you pfhucked up. Everything was going so well and suddenly she disappeared. "Chicks," you mutter and swear off them forever (until the next night).

Do you want to know what happened? Well, unfortunately you blew it on two counts. Not only did you move a little too close to her a second time without waiting for her turn to close the distance. You also exhibited a slight flinch of surprise when she actually reached over and touched your jacket. That was the time when you should have, at the very least, moved toward her touch. Even better, at that point, since she was teasing, you could have used it as an excuse to playfully grab her hand and not let go until she gave the hair back to you.

> Your responding "guy sex signal" should always match the intensity and
> style of her signal. Whether the lady you've just fallen in lust with is the
> preacher's daughter at the church social or a broad whose tombstone will
> read, "The only time she ever slept alone," always take your cue from the
> lady.

How Close Should You Stand?

"Well, how am I supposed to know how close is *too close*?" you ask.
The answer is not easy, but the solution is. First, the hard part.
Every woman's definition of personal space is a little different, and
invading that sacred territory without "an invitation" makes her
feel ambushed.

Now, the easy part, no sweat. To determine her particular pa-
rameters, simply start your conversation a little too far away.
Gradually close the distance between you and the moment you see
her nose move back, even a millimeter, back up 2 millimeters. Now
you're at the perfect spot to excite but not invade.

Unfortunately, in real life, we can't turn the clock back a few
hours and do something all over again the right way. In a book,
however, we can! Roll back the tape. You're back at the bar. We
pick up with . . .

"By now you and a very turned-on flirtatious Ashley are leaning
slightly toward each other to close the distance between you.
Everything's going great . . ." You're keeping your distance as you
continue to chat with her and showing your appreciation of everything she says.

Remember, guys, this is the 21st century. You no longer need to
impress a woman by telling her how well you hack and slash your
way through the corporate jungle to bag a big paycheck. Today's
woman probably earns just as much as you, and she's going to be

more impressed by the size of your smile than the size of your wallet. That was your dad's and granddad's game. Put your effort into showing how impressed you are by her.

Step Four: The Leaning In

As you execute this exercise with savoir-faire, you will see her begin to almost melt toward you. Like a magnet, you will draw toward her. It is as though a retractable tape measure were calculating the space between your noses and it was slowly getting shorter and shorter. You can see another example of this in our discussion of the "leaning in" sex signal.

The last time, you leaned too close. This time, you do it right. You may follow by leaning in toward her—*but only by the number of millimeters she has initiated.*

Now your entire body is focused on her as hers is on you. It is as though you have shut out the rest of the people in the bar and have hung out a "do not disturb" sign. You are looking deeply into each other's eyes as you converse. Your eyes and hers begin to traverse down to each other's shoulders and arms.

How to Get Those Seductive "Bedroom Eyes"

I promised you I'd discuss the second part of the campaign, which is to win her with your eyes. Here it is. When a man truly starts to fall in love, he is lulled by good feelings. Then his eyes start to wander lovingly over his beloved's face, hair, and eyes. His eyes do a little ski jump off her nose and then swirl around her lips. When you're looking at her lovingly like this, your pupils become larger. Thus, you have those sexy "bedroom eyes." Note that this technique works better in darkened rooms than in bright light, which reduces the size of your pupils.

This pleasurable voyage of the eyes of turned-on couples who feel completely comfortable with each other was recognized as early as 1977 by a male researcher who conducted a study called "Gaze and Mutual Gaze in Social Encounters." It was reported in the professional journal *American Scientist*.[50] He proved that gazing deeply into a woman's eyes can even be the spark that turns her on and makes her think that maybe she's falling in love with you.

Incidentally, stay north of her neck. Copping a peek at any part of her body below her chin is rude this early.

As you lean in toward each other, let your eyes soften. You can emulate a curious phenomenon that happens to a man's eyes when he starts to truly love someone. Let your eyes start to wander lovingly over the woman's face, hair, and eyes. Have them do a little ski jump off her nose and then swirl around her lips. Occasionally, take a courageous trip to her neck and shoulders. (Her boobs are still off-limits. You have no passport to travel to that territory—yet!)

Step Five: Moving in Synchrony

The final step to becoming "a couple" for the evening, for the night, or for a lifetime, is to begin moving in sequence with her. As she lifts her glass to her face, lift your glass to yours. As she leans with an elbow on the bar, do the same. If she's standing and puts a foot on the step, do the same. It's an old NLP, or neuro-linguistic programming trick, when done consciously. But it happens instinctively with people who genuinely do think and feel alike.

You have a choice here. You can either "mirror copy" or "cross copy" the lady's movements. The latter term means that when she uses her left hand to pick up a napkin, you use your left as well. This kind of synchrony is less obvious than mirror imaging. Whichever you choose, you must be very deft at this game or you run the danger of being detected.

Why move in synchrony with her? It gives her the impression that you are on the same wavelength—that you think alike and feel alike. (If you like a chick's body, you probably don't give a hoot if she wants to save the rain forest from parasites or not. She does.) Keep in mind that it is far more important to a woman than it is to you that you have similar basic values, beliefs, reactions, and ways of looking at the world.

In a university study, researchers fixed men and women up on blind dates.[51] Some of the women were told, confidentially, that their blind dates would have attitudes toward life very similar to their own. Others were told they would not. (Both were lies for the sake of science.)

However, when the women were quizzed afterward about how much they liked their dates, the women who were previously told their attitudes were *similar*, liked them a lot more—even in cases when they were really very dissimilar, thus demonstrating that a woman is predisposed toward a man who thinks like she does.

Dr. Perper offered the following observation:

> "Once synchronized, couples can stay in synchrony seemingly indefinitely, until the bar closes, until they finish dinner and drinks and must leave, or until their train reaches wherever it is going; to put it another way, until the business of the outside world intervenes and causes their interaction to stop."[52]

We saw synchronicity at work in the photo illustrating *The Copycat* sex signal. Ashley was either unconsciously copying Matt's movements, or she knew precisely what she was doing to turn him on.

Let's get back to you and Ashley in the first scene. Unfortunately, she blew you off before you ever reached this stage, and as a result, you felt like a failure, a lamebrain whose personality just didn't measure up. Wrong! You just didn't obey Mother Nature, who decrees that *in order to become part of a couple, you must follow the laws of nature and respond appropriately to her sex signals.*

Skeptical? I was too. But, since I am constantly on the road dining alone at restaurants, I have become a shameless people watcher. I always get a table with a good view of the bar, and I've watched countless numbers of encounters progress from a couple's just meeting to their walking out the door arm in arm. And all the steps were completed in order, just like closing a zipper. Go ahead, get out those very dark glasses, the kind some folks wear to nude beaches. Don them the next time you happen to find yourself in a singles situation. You'll see. Dr. Perper has the right prescription.

All the studies on initial attraction establish that attraction to a stranger is strongly dependent on the perceived degree of similarity between the subjects. And, one of the best ways to make her perceive that you're alike is to move in sequence with her. The final step is riveting to watch. Couples who are on the road to making it get on each other's wavelength so precisely that they start to mirror, or move in synchrony, with each other. To emulate this, reach for your drink when she does, put your glass back on the bar when she does, etc.

Try it! Just one night out, decide that every time you talk with a chick, you're going to copy her movements. (Within reason, of course. If she powders her nose, don't ask to borrow her puff.) See how warm and fuzzy it makes her feel toward you.

Practice makes perfect! Rehearse these five steps with women you are not particularly attracted to. Once you experience the success the moves bring you, use them more comfortably with women you might not have approached before.

Too many men trip themselves up by doing the two-step jig when the band's playin' the slower and sexier music. If you have designs on ever seeing her bedroom ceiling, here is what you must do, in this order, step by step.

- Acknowledge her signal or her response to yours.

- Respond creatively and with the same intensity she has.

- Approach her appropriately.

- Say something neutral and preferably complimentary to open the conversation.

Then, while talking, follow nature's courtship dance. Here's a review of the five step waltz.

1. Turn just your head at first.

2. Gradually rotate your torso as she does.

3. Turn your full body slowly toward her.

4. Lean in closer when she does.

5. Gradually synchronize your movements.

24

Your Opening Lines

You'll notice, I hope, that I said, "lines," not "line." Every woman is different. Face it, the chick with orange hair in the leather micro-skirt and the debutante with a French twist in the Versace pantsuit are not going to go for the same guy just because he has a great opening line. And you're wasting your money on any book or tape that tells you otherwise. Besides, it's not so much what you say as *how* you say it. Since the question of "What's a good opening line?" is such a perennial—in fact, it's an invasive weed that I can't kill—I've made it my hobby over the years to ask my girlfriends about some of the best and the worst they've heard.

The worst opening lines concern a woman's physical appearance such as "What's a beautiful woman like you doing in a place like this?" or "What's a beautiful girl like you doing without a date tonight?" And *definitely* never open with comments about her body. A woman wants to think you are more interested in her personality, her mind.

Especially revealing into that pretty little head of hers was an ad I once saw for Dewar's scotch. It was a rear shot of two women jogging along the beach with four of the most beautiful buns that sand ever stuck to. One of the women was proudly saying to the other, "He loves me for my *mind*, and he drinks Dewars."

Now, this poses a problem. If you're supposed to like her for her mind and haven't even met her yet, how are you supposed to know what her mind is like? Here's the tactic. You ask her a question—any question: for example, "What time is it?" or "Do you by any chance know the bartender's (or party host's, or event organizer's) name?" Or ask her what she's drinking. If it's beer, you can say, "Oh, why do you like Heineken?" (or whatever she's drinking). If it's wine or a mixed drink, ask her about that. In other words, make small talk. Remember, she's not judging you on what you say as long as it doesn't involve her. It's how you say it.

Then, when she gives her answer, give evidence of a growing interest in her. Keep her engaged in conversation so she gets the idea that you are fascinated by what she says.

"Wait," I can hear you say. "Your ad promised me the world's *best* opening line." And, yes, I promise to give it to you. The world's all time best opening line? Maestro, the trumpet-blare please: You stand up straight and tall. You look friendly and confident. You smile at the lady, look her right in the eyes, and in a warm, inviting (but not salacious), charismatic voice, you say, "Hello, my name is _____."

Gentlemen, upon my honor, nothing beats this line. It's preferred by 10 out of every 10 women, age 16 to 66, that I've ever asked. It has stood the test of time. Even Grandma said she used to prefer that one.

"What do I say once I'm past the first sentence?" you ask.

Leave it to science. Researchers asked the same question. My all-time favorite study in this area is called "Behavioral Assessment of Social Competence in Males,"[53] in other words, "What helps a guy score with women?"

The researchers chose two groups of men to participate in their study: guys who scored and guys who didn't. The guys who scored were designated "winners." These guys were invited to many parties, were popular with women, and were well liked by all. These fellows dated a lot and were able to make it with women.

Men in the second group were flops with women. They tried, but they never got to first base. The researchers ruthlessly and candidly dubbed these guys "losers." These fellows wanted desperately to date, but they were either hesitant to ask a woman out or were continually getting turned down.

Since the two groups of men were equally good-looking, researchers set about isolating what made women go for the winners and avoid the losers. They put the men through a series of tests.

The venue for the first test was at a dance. All the men were told was to ask a woman to dance. The women (who were in on the study) were directed to respond by saying, "I'm not really much of a dancer."

Upon hearing this, invariably, the winners, the cool guys, simply laughed, and responded with variations of "I'm not either. Shall we sit this one out?" and began talking with her. *The winners did not take her answer as a rejection of them but simply as a statement of fact.*

The losers responded with a variety of "Oh," "Er," "Um, well," and the like and then they gave up. In short, they interpreted the female's answer as a rebuff.

In the second test, researchers taped conversations between the girls and the winners and between the same girls and the losers. This time, the women did not know it was a study. The guys were told to chat with a woman for a while and eventually ask her for a date.

The big difference between the losers, who almost always got turned down for the date, and the winners, who received a lot of "yes" answers, was a simple matter of keeping the *rhythm* of the conversation going.

The cool guys chatted, asking questions, and as soon as the woman answered those questions, they'd pick up the slump by offering their own views or experiences. They asked the women more questions to keep the conversation going. The bottom line? They permitted very few pauses in the conversation. They kept the rhythm and the electricity going.

The poor losers weren't any less interesting in what they had to say. They just had no sensitivity as to the timing. There were more awkward gaps in the conversation. They paused too long, or hemmed and hawed before answering. The "musicality" of the exchange was off, which made the women uncomfortable.

Researchers also clocked the men's answers to questions the women asked. The winners gave much longer answers. The losers often muttered just a "yes" or a "no." After a couple of those, the conversation had nowhere to go. But the girls did. The losers heard a lot of remarks like, "Well, nice talking to you. (Sure!) See ya around." The winners heard a lot of remarks like, "I'm really looking forward to seeing you again."

Stamp out one-word answers to questions! Elaborate, even if you think what you're saying is superfluous. Don't let there be long pauses. Ask her questions about herself. Practice sounding enthusiastic and energetic. That translates into "happy and confident."

Your First Conversation

Women are like the old eight-track music tapes when they got twisted. They can run on all eight tracks at once. You're chatting with a chick you've just met, and she's running the old eight-track on you. The first track is her judging how you look. The second track is her judging how you move. The third track is her judging how you dress. The fourth track is her judging how you sound. The fifth track is her judging your character. The sixth track is judging your probable job. The seventh track is judging how much you like her. And *finally*, only the eighth track is listening to what you have to say. So that we don't leave any stone unturned, let's deal with your first conversation with her and what it reveals about you.

You may think you're just having an innocent conversation about, let's say, the homeless, taxes to support public schools, or the minimum wage. Sounds safe enough, doesn't it? No way! She's listening to find out how compassionate you are.

Say she asks you about your family. You think she cares about Mom and Sis—whom she's never even met? No, she's listening to find out whether you're a mama's boy, a cruel heartless man who would someday treat her just as mean, or something in between those. Remember, almost every question has a hidden motive. En garde!

Suppose you're talking with a divorced woman who has two young children at home. She's bound to ask you, openly or cir-cuitously, how you feel about kids. Be ready for questions as obvi-ous as "Do you like children?" and "Where do you see yourself five years from now?" Your answer could be the skeleton key to her heart, soul, and body—or a skull and crossbones on your forehead.

Her eyes are wide open, observing your every move—especially how you treat the bartender when he asks you if you'd like another round or the drunk who bumps into you and spills your drink. Think "compassion," man, "compassion." Remember that she's beating the bushes for your beliefs and values from the first "hello."

Keep your ears finely tuned and show solidarity. Every grain of difference between you at this early stage will feel as large as a stone in her eye, blinding her to your greatness. She's Republican? There's no need to highlight how active you are in the Democratic Party. She hates Laurel and Hardy and the Three Stooges? There's no need to tell her about your awesome collection of slapstick videos. She's pro-choice? There's no need to tell her you got the gold medal for your high-school debating team with your cogent pro-life argument. Mark my words, gentlemen, even your minor values and beliefs are major to a woman right off the bat.[54]

Oh, and one last warning. Be careful the first time you mention one of your extracurricular activities. The health club? (Mention it twice and you're a health freak.) Church? (Mention it twice and you're a religious fanatic.) The beach? (Mention it twice and you're a beach bum.) Think balance, man, balance. Still make the first mention a true representation of your character, or, at least the type of character you want to portray.

The Dozen Best Ways to Break the Ice

I always tell guys who ask about icebreakers to melt the ice the way they'd melt real ice—with warmth, not words. But there's something about the rational guy brain that wants to know what to say. So here goes.

The first thing to understand is that women don't listen the same way you do, to facts. They are listening *between the lines* to see what they can find out about you. They're looking to see if you are "boyfriend" or "husband" material, which brings us to the age-old question of "What the heck does a woman really want?"

An anthropologist studied 37 societies around the world to discover the answer. Wherever she went, she got the same four qualities a woman is on the lookout for in a man.[55] From Paris to Pago Pago, from New York to New Guinea, they all want these qualities in their guys—and they'll be listening for them in everything you say at first.

The Four Qualities Every Woman Wants in a Man

A.   Resources. Read essentially "money," but education, intelligence, and good taste fall into this category too. It's just her genes acting up again, wanting to know you can take care of her and eventual offspring

B.   Status. This doesn't mean you have to be the CEO of your own company or be the class president, but she wants to know that other people respect you too.

C.   Physical strength. This is a throwback to a day when a man had to protect his woman and the bambino from marauding enemy tribes. And don't forget to bring home the buffalo burgers. (Hold the chips.)

D.   Emotionally caring. She wants to know you care about people (mainly her someday) and will listen to people's problems (especially hers).

How to Show Her You've Got "The Right Stuff"

So, how do you express all this without going up to her and saying, "Hi, I'm rich, strong, Harold, and all my admiring friends want the best for me; I thought I'd come over here and listen to your problems."

It's not what you tell her that makes you sound good; it's what you *don't* tell her and she can read between the lines.

Chicks don't listen to what you're saying as much as they do to what you're not. Never brag, but learn the subtle art of *hinting* at your own magnificence.

A little more subtlety, please. So . . .

1. Compliment something she's wearing, especially a piece of jewelry, and ask her where she bought it. So that it doesn't come off as just as an excuse, tell her you're looking for a birthday present for, let's say, your sister. Now here's the part that makes you look good. Tell her you were looking in Tiffany's (or whatever the most expensive jewelry store in your town is) and, darn, you just couldn't find anything. That shows letters A (resources) and D (caring). She also starts fantasizing about receiving some diamond earrings herself from Tiffany's.

2. A currently popular film is always safe conversational fodder, but find out her opinion on it first and make sure yours agrees with it. Then quote a review from the *New York Times* (which you can get free on line at NYTimes.com so bone up ahead of time). This approach will make you seem intelligent and well-read, which is part of letter A (resources).

3. A local charity event is a triple whammy. Check the paper. Talking about one makes it sound as if you have resources (letter A), have status (letter B), and are emotionally caring (letter D).

4. Ask her about her job, which makes you sound emotionally caring (letter D). This is necessary—but make sure you don't ask in a way that could be construed as your interest in *her* status or money. Heaven forbid your turning the tables!

5. The most important overlooked turn-on for the 21st-century woman is alluding to a way you can help her professionally Maybe you can introduce her to people who

could be beneficial to her. This shows your status (letter B). Or you might provide some insight into a professional question she's wrestling with at the moment, showing that you are caring (letter D).

6. Just toss off sentences like, "When I was shoveling my grandmother's driveway the other day . . ." You come off as physically strong (letter C) and emotionally caring (letter D).

7. Find a way to ask about the people in her life (no, not her boyfriend). They are very important to her, and she loves talking about them. This makes you sound emotionally caring (letter D). Then, you might casually mention yours, thus demonstrating status (letter B). And, while you're at it, throw in some heavyweight activity you did with your buddies and thus show your physical strength (letter C).

8. Ask her about her favorite restaurants. Then drop the names of some of yours (no, not Fridays, even though the food is tasty). Go first-class here. This gives a high mark in the resources category (letter A) in terms of both money and good taste (in addition to whetting her appetite for a fine dining experience).

9. Try to get the subject around to her pets if she has any. If she has a cat, chances are she's bonkers over it—so arm yourself with some good cat-care facts. Only super caring men (letter D) would know how to care for a cat!

10. Did you ever slug a guy for insulting your sister or your girlfriend? Did you ever get into a fight for some honorable cause—not not a bar brawl? Allude to it sometime to show you are caring (letter D) and physically strong (let-

ter C). But make sure she knows you're not ordinarily the fighting kind.

11. Here's the last and most important conversational ploy: Listen very carefully to her as she speaks and, whatever subject she even touches on—even via a word here or there out of the blue about something, pick up on it and ask her about it. That shows that you are very emotionally caring (letter D), and that you are capable of listening between the lines.

12. Whatever subject you wind up discussing, quote something that you read about in (take your pick of the following publications): *Forbes, US News and World Report*, the *Economist*, the *Wall Street Journal*, or the *Investor's Business Daily*. You know what all that shows. If she's more the literary type, quote any of your favorite books (except this one).

Be Prepared to Answer the Most Important Question She'll Ask

The most important thing, by far, is how you answer the inevitable question: "And what do you do?" As I said earlier, in spite of all the progress we've made toward equality in earning, it's still tucked away in many women's genes that you have to either earn more, be smarter, or be just plain "better" (whatever that means). Even during the heyday of feminism, mothers were reading fairy tales like *Cinderella* to their daughters. (Cinderella married the handsome prince.) Or they took their daughters to see feature length cartoons like *Thumbalina*. (Thumbalina married the handsome prince.) And there's no end in sight. Little girls today are seeing Disney's *Beauty and the Beast*. Well, the beast isn't so handsome, but he's still a rich prince.

You can be sure that the little girl, still trapped inside even the most accomplished and wealthy of women today, still retains her dream that "someday, my prince will come." As the years go by, she has probably expanded her definition of "prince." He doesn't necessarily need to be wealthy. He could be the dedicated doctor prince, the principled politician prince, the sensitive starving artist prince, the talented carpenter prince. In any event, whatever her vision is of her prince, the closer your answer to "What do you do?" is to that, the better chance you'll have with her.

Now, you obviously have no control over what her ultimate dream is or how close your life comes to that dream. But this much is certain: Her prince is proud. He is confident, and he loves his own life. When she asks you what you do for a living, whatever your answer, respond with enthusiasm. Don't talk overly long about your work, but make it evident that you are dedicated and love your own life. (Then, don't forget to ask her about *her* life and *her* work!)

Meeting to Mating
(How to Win the Dating Game)

25

Shrewd Dating Strategies

Many a brave knave gets a bad case of butterfly guts when it comes to popping the question "Will you go out with me?" Why? It's the old salesman's malady, *fear of rejection*. So many men never ask. No guts, no glory.

Other men, a tad *too* confident of their own charm and the lady's acceptance, bestow the invitation to spend an evening in their incomparable company too quickly—only to be shocked by her brush-off.

Several years ago, I was at a party and spotted a fabulous specimen of raw male sex appeal. He bore a striking resemblance to a young Jack Nicholson on a good day. I smiled at him, and he smiled back. At that moment, I vowed I was going to meet him. I started conniving. Perhaps I'd try to finagle an introduction from the host of the party. Or maybe I'd cough up a corny line like "Haven't we met before?" I even contemplated the desperate move of waiting until he was seated and then "just happening" to trip and fall into his lap.

As I was ruminating about my options, he walked right up to me and said he'd like me to go to dinner with him the next evening.

My surprised answer? "No, thanks." And I was sincere. It was too much too soon. He didn't know anything about me. How could he have known about my scintillating personality, my incredible uniqueness, my extraordinary acumen, my resplendence, and my rare humility?

And, worse, I didn't know anything about him. He may have looked like Jack Nicholson, but he could have had the nasty habits of Jack the Ripper—or Jack Nicholson in *The Shining*.

When and How to Ask Her Out

In real estate, a well-known adage is "location, location, location." Well, in asking for a date, it's "timing, timing, timing." When should you ask for milady's company? Let her feel she got a date with you "the old-fashioned way," by *earning* it. Otherwise, your company is as valued as a screen door on a submarine.

Sometimes, my actress friends are cast in Broadway shows as extras—which is still a great honor. But they are never as excited about the gig if the director just "typecast" them. Being typecast merely means that they *look* the part. It has nothing to do with their acting ability. And no woman, no matter how beautiful she is, or isn't, wants to feel that you just asked her out because of her looks.

There is a second reason to wait before asking her out. Because a woman is investing an evening of her precious time in you, she wants to know she's going to enjoy it. So, like an actor auditioning for an important producer, give her a bigger sample of you before asking her out.

This does not mean making a laundry list of your good qualities. Nor does it mean airing your dirty laundry concerning your last six failed relationships. It's more along the lines of making natural conversation and letting your wit and intelligence speak for themselves. Try to balance the conversation, revealing yourself a bit more while keeping the focus on her. That gives her the input she needs to make the "go/no go decision."

> Since a woman wants to feel she is the recipient of your awe and admiration, as opposed to your lust and lewdness, ask her questions about herself. Then, when she says something especially revealing, show how fascinated you are by what she's saying. *That's* the time to ask her out. "Oh, you know all about 12th-century dental practices. Gee, that's fascinating! I'd love to continue this discussion say, uh—next Saturday night."

Postscript: Don't reveal *too* much. A little mystery also fans the flames of passion.

To Her, It's Not a Date—It's an Audition!

Guys, my heart goes out to you. A female, on your first date, misses nothing. I mean *nothing*. No analyst ever examined a patient's mentality as much as a woman will analyze you on everything you say, everything you do, and everything she thinks you're thinking. She picks up on your every word, your every movement. She scrutinizes how you look and how she *assumes* you feel, and tries to piece together your life history. When she's got a fix on that, she fantasizes about your future. Does she want to be a part of it? "Long range," "short range," or "fat chance!"

No crashed commercial airliner ever got the scrutiny you're going to get as you innocently sit across the restaurant table happily chatting about this and that. Be on your toes, because now is the time that you are being auditioned to play a leading role in her bedroom. In days gone by, it used to be that a woman had to "feel in love" to go to bed with someone. Now it just has to "feel right."

What makes it "feel right"? Quite simply, if she feels your character is in sync with hers and you make her feel special. You must do this from the first pitch to the bottom of the ninth.

The Proven Best Thing to Do on the First Date

Where *you* would probably like to go on your first date with her (a football game), where *she* would like to go (dinner at an upscale restaurant), and where you *should* go (information pending) for maximum sex appeal are three different places. Sure, you'd probably like the sporting event, because if she turned out to be a dud, you could at least enjoy the game. She'd like the restaurant, because, in addition to a great meal, she'd have the opportunity, during the conversation, to evaluate you as someone who could possibly be part of her future. But if your goal is (as the fact that you're reading this attests) to bed the lass and possibly someday wed the lass, that is not the best choice.

There is compelling evidence that she will be more turned on to you if you place her in a "scary, emotional, or vulnerable" situation. You don't need to lock her in the trunk of your car and tell her you're going to drive it over a cliff. A scary movie will do. Or, if she is a fan of Gregorian chants or heavy metal, an evening of chants or a Metallica concert will qualify as an emotional situation.

Research has shown a strong link between emotional arousal and sexual attraction. Have you ever wondered why, in all the great love stories depicted on the screen, on the stage, and in novels, the lovers or wannabe lovers face a great challenge together? Often, a towering inferno, a jungle of prehistoric beasts, a tornado, or a motley selection of evil forces threatens to tear the couple asunder. Did it ever cross your mind that they might not be lovers, or even want to be, if it weren't for the immense adversity they had to tackle together? I mean, what would be the big deal about Romeo dating Juliet if the Montegues didn't want to kill all the Capulets?

Consider this: More office romances start in workplaces that have atrocious bosses than in offices filled with happy campers. Potential lovers placed in an emotional, stirring, or vulnerable situation are more apt to be attracted to each other because "It's you and me, Babe, against this big bad boss."

At least one study, reported upon in the *Journal of Personality and Social Psychology* and called "Evidence for Heightened Sexual Attraction Under Conditions of High Anxiety," proved the connection between fear and sexual attraction.[56] Subjects who had volunteered for the study (without knowing what it involved) were brought into a laboratory where a male and a female researcher were sitting. The researchers told half the volunteers they were going to receive a very severe shock. The other half were told that they would receive an extremely mild shock.

Each subject was then introduced to another researcher of the opposite sex who stayed for a few minutes and then left. After his or her departure, the researcher of the same sex asked the subject's opinion of the person who just left. The results? The girls who sat quaking in their shoes and shuddering about the severe shock to come rated the guy who just left as much sexier than did the girls who were going to get the mild shock.

Studies like these show that when a woman is feeling a strong emotion, such as fear, she's more apt to be turned on to you. Why do women experience these whacko reactions? As is the case with most whacko reactions, the answer goes back to drugs—in this case phenylethylamine, or PEA, the naturally produced drug discussed earlier. Fear produces the same high that shoots through our veins in the early stages of infatuation.

Barring the physical, go for something that's emotionally exciting for her. Does she love opera? If so take her to the opera. (How about *Madame Butterfly*? That leaves everybody sobbing at the end.) Does she love movies? Take her to a movie. (Have you seen any good horror films lately?) Does she like amusement parks? Take her to the amusement park (and be sure to go on the death-defying, killer-diller, triple-twist roller coaster).

> Obviously you're not going to tell the lady she's going to receive a severe shock by dropping hot candle wax on her nipples (unless she's one of those kinky gals who's into that sort of thing). But science tells us that if your first experience together is stirring, your date will transfer the strong emotions to you.
>
> Physical activities that get you moving around are also good. Physical activities that get you moving around *and* touching each other are even better. Unless you'd look like a cow on ice, dancing is a good choice.

Stamping Out Piggy Male Manners

Most men are a little fuzzy about manners. It comes with the territory. I can hear you now. You're grousing, "Criminy, I answered an ad saying, 'What if you never heard the word *no* from a woman again?' and you're going to tell me I have to extend my pinky when drinking from a cup?"

No, of course not. There's no need to sweat the small stuff, but you want to eliminate the gross fouls that turn female umpires off—such as talking with your mouth full, using the wrong fork, picking a piece of painful roast beef out of your back tooth with the edge of a Sweet'n Low packet, and forcing your way onto the bus before the people get off—and then, to top it off, not giving the little old lady your seat. Honest, the good manners you exhibit on a date rank right up there with great sexual technique.

A few hints: After parking in the restaurant parking lot, swiftly leap around to her side of the car, open the door, and extend your hand to help her out. She'll be impressed.

As you cross the street, offer her your arm, lest she, wobbling in her painful little shoes, should trip. For that matter, even if she's wearing sneakers and says, "Ah, you don't need to do that," she'll secretly appreciate it.

Oops, you spot a little doggie-doo-doo by the curb? Non-chalantly steer milady's path so her tootsies don't get soiled. (Do *not* then bring your gallant deed to her attention by saying, "Boy, I sure saved you from that shit, huh?") As you enter the restaurant, you, of course, hold the door for her.

"Nice," she'll think. As you head for your table, pull her chair out before seating yourself. Now, knowing you're an all-class dude, she'll start having X-rated thoughts, such as whether you're a "boxer shorts" or a "briefs" man.

The lady will probably be carrying a purse. If you want to know how you're doing so far, check to see if she instinctively moves it to the side you're not walking on so there is no obstruction between the two of you. If she moves it, she likes you. If she leaves it between you, it's as if she's using it for protection.

Now you're at the restaurant. As I mentioned before, if the maitre d' isn't there to do it, pull the chair out for her. When it comes time to order, you should ask her what she would like for dinner and then give both your orders to the waiter. She'll be purring. And if you say, "the lady will have" (as opposed to "she will have), she'll begin imagining peeling either your boxer shorts or your briefs off with her teeth.

I kid you not. Manners matter.

The All-Important Dinner Date

No matter what you do on your first date with her, you're eventually going to wind up putting the feedbag on together. Where should you take her for this first ceremonial breaking of bread?

Alas, what impressionable creatures we women are! Why we get upset when you mentally undress us is beyond my comprehension. You are, in a sense, looking at the *real* us, without the trappings. Women are much more impressed by a man's clothes than you are by ours, and we are also impressed (or depressed) by the atmosphere of the places you take us.

Before you make a decision, let me clear up one misconception. You may think you're being nice by asking her where she'd like to go, letting her decide. She may even enjoy choosing the place. But there are two big negatives. First and worst, it makes you look androgynous. Take charge, man. You make the reservations—and don't forget to confirm them! It will make you look real bad to her if your table isn't ready on time just because Robert DiNiro made a reservation right after you did and you got aced. Better yet, try to "be known" to the maitre d' so he welcomes you by name. (It's astounding what good memories a maitre d' will develop if your handshake was padded with a little green the last time you were there.)

Now, two factors affect your choice of restaurant. The first is your realization of how superficial a woman can be in her judgments. In fact, researchers showed pictures of men to a group of women.[57] Sometimes, the men were photographed in lavish, luxuriant (read "rich") rooms. Other times, the cameras showed them in dilapidated, dumpy settings. To isolate the *setting* as the variable, in this particular study, the pictures were of the very same men dressed in precisely the same way.

It is with some embarrassment that I tell you that the men in the lavish looking house were judged more attractive than the men in the dumpy house. Women will definitely transfer their feelings about whatever setting you are in to their feelings about you.

One of the advantageous things about sitting across the table from a woman is that you can get a real good read on how much she likes you. Here, Jade, a very sophisticated woman, is using a sub-liminal sex signal on you.

Well, it's not too subtle, is it?

Like the sirens who lured sailors to their death by their beautiful singing, some women will lure men across the room to talk to them by their sensuously caressing a glass or cylindrical object like a pen.

UNDERCOVER SEX SIGNAL #23:

The Sexy Pet

If you see a woman across the room looking at you and not smiling, you might not think she wants you to approach. But if you take careful note of her hands, you may see she is running a finger around her wineglass. It is not out of boredom. She might even be imagining that she is caressing you. In this picture, Jade has chosen to caress her glass with her pointing finger, figuring that her middle finger or ring finger would be just too obvious.

At other times, a woman uses *the sexy pet* by fondling a pen suggestively or running her fingers up and down the *stem* of a wineglass.

If you are already conversing with a woman, it is likely to be a contrived move when she slowly and seductively runs her finger around the rim or up and down the stem of a glass when talking with you. Almost any object can be used suggestively—a pen, a utensil, a swizzle stick, etc.

Taking this deficit in the female psyche—judging you by the place you take her—into account, take her to an eatery that reflects the personality you'd like to project. In fact, if the lady is really worth it, take her to the most upscale restaurant in that genre that you can find, but not one where you're going to have to worry about which of six forks to choose from.

Do you like to be thought of as artistic? Take her to a restaurant where (relatively rich) artists go. Do you want her to think of you as a successful businessman? Take her to a restaurant where (relatively rich) businessmen go. Do you want her to think of you as a cool dude? Take her to a restaurant where (relatively rich) cool dudes go. Would you like her to think of you as a hippie? Take her to a restaurant where (relatively rich) hippies go.

Ok, ok, so that's an oxymoron, but you get the idea.

There is one exception. Even if you want her to think of you as a jock, do *not* take her to a sports bar—unless of course, she's used to hanging out there anyway. In which case, she's a rarity; so make her a keeper.

If the lass has class, you should take her to a really fine dining establishment the first time you go out with her. Since, however, the tiny provisions and exorbitant prices at some restaurants will leave you both hungry and broke, you don't want her to become accustomed to that style. On your next date, therefore, avoid any mention of where she'd like to go.

She might already be suffering delusions that other expensive restaurants are going to become among her regular haunts. You may handle such a distressing situation in this manner. Don't just choose an inexpensive "normal" restaurant the next time. Instead, take her to some charming (read "inexpensive") restaurant serving ethnic cuisine. Tell her you've been reading about, say, Vietnamese food, and can't wait to try it. (The average dinner price in all the Vietnamese restaurants I know is in the single digits.)

Then for date three, back to Les Expensivo. Next date El Cheapo. And soon your eclectic taste in food will even include a Fridays and Taco Bell, in time to make the movie. But, by then, the two of you should be making it, and the choice of restaurant will probably be the least of your problems.

> Bonus hint: Try to get her to order a chocolate dessert. Some say there is a minor link between sexual arousal and chocolate. More accurate is "the chocolate link." If she's watching her weight but lets herself go and pigs out on a high-calorie monster, it means she's feeling pretty loose.

Incidentally, there is a strong argument for taking her to a quiet restaurant that is darkly lit. Women aren't the only ones who look better in candlelight. Men also look more alluring, more mysterious. Their eyes get sexier due to the pupils' opening up in the darkness. (Bedroom eyes, remember?)

Now, all this talk of restaurants brings me to two oft-asked questions: "Should I let her pay for the dinner?" My short answer is "No." "How about letting her leave the tip?" many men ask. Again, the answer is "No." Say it however you like. Whether it's the tough guy's, "Your money's no good in here, Babe" or the more refined "How kind of you to offer, but I wouldn't hear of it" (or anything in between), she'll appreciate it.

I know such an approach may be viewed by some as unjust, inequitable, and antiquated. It may even run counter to everything the lady *says* she prefers. But you already know that every woman has at least a bit of the romantic in her, a feeling that "someday my prince will come along on a great white horse, he'll scoop me up, and we'll ride off into the sunset together and live happily ever after." And what kind of a prince ever lets a woman pay. Or even go dutch? (On later dates, after you're friends and lovers, it's another matter. Even then, however, pretend to be a little "disturbed" that she's picking up the check.)

Kissing, Calling, and Other Follow-up Strategies

It's hard to believe that the male of the same species that planted the American flag on the moon still wonders if he should plant a kiss on a woman's lips on the first date. Here's where everything you've learned up to this point comes into play. Have you kept count of the many undercover sex signals she's been hurling your way? Has she been smiling? Has she been leaning in toward you? Has she turned her palms toward you? Has she brushed her hair back while talking with you? Has she run a finger around a glass? Has she put a swizzle stick in her mouth while listening to you? Those are just six signs. There are 19 other nonverbal cues that show she'd like you to take her in your arms. Soon, reading them will become second nature.

Otherwise brilliant and accomplished American males are flummoxed by questions like "How long should I wait before calling her again?" and "Should I tell her at the end of the first date that I'd like to see her again?" Let's say you see her Saturday night. You like her—a lot. You want to see her again the following Saturday. So you're wondering about your best call-back strategy.

Pieced together from conversations I've had with the many hundreds of women in my classes, here are the options and what each is likely to make her think.

Should I call later the same night? Unless she left some life-support medicine in your car, it makes you look too lonely and anxious.

Should I call Sunday? If you do, you risk looking like you think she's the only game in town for you.

Should I call Monday? Nah, that's being too predictable

Should I call Tuesday? It's not the most tactical strategy. Let her get a tad concerned.

Should I call Wednesday? By that time, she'll be getting really worried that you might not call.

The most tactical time to call is late Wednesday afternoon at work, or at her home if you really do want to see her the following week. (At one shameful time in our history, all females were reading a ridiculous book called *The Rules*, a book that set relationships back half a century. It said, "Don't accept a date for Saturday night later than Wednesday." What a travesty!)

A super-cool move: Call her office Saturday night after your date and leave a voice-mail message saying, "I had a great time—I'll call you this week." Then don't call until Thursday. If she likes you already, that'll drive her nuts over you.

Now, even better, is to call her on Thursday, not for the upcoming weekend, but for the following weekend. That will keep her guessing and yet still interested. (Not to mention it permits you to juggle two ladies at the same time. I call it "flextime" dating.)

26

Big-Time Help

(If You Suspect You Have
a "Big-Deal" Problem)

If you suspect serious shyness with women is your problem, it's time to get serious about shyness—because shyness is serious business.

Women are attracted to men who have a healthy ego. In fact, Madonna, when being interviewed on what attracted her to the father of her first baby, said the first thing she noticed was his totally unshakable self-confidence, bordering on arrogance.

Shyness has many insidious side effects. Did you know that shy men, on the occasion of a first meeting, are considered to be less intelligent than they are? Furthermore, they often consider themselves to be much less attractive than they really are. Due to their shyness, they never feel complete and never attain a satisfactory "sense of self."[58] Shy men have difficulty making friends, they date less, and, when they do, they're forever botching up the friendship or love affair. Shy men are even less likely than those who suffer from other types of anxiety problems to find a partner and get married.[59]

Shyness doesn't just screw men up in the dating department. Shy men are slower to get into a satisfactory career. And when they do, their careers are more unstable right on through mid-life. They seldom find a job that utilizes their real talents.[60]

Have you heard enough to get serious about ridding your life of this blight? Well, let me just add this: Shy men suffer more from self-deprecatory thoughts,[61] inhibited behavior,[62] loneliness,[63] anxiety attacks,[64] and depression[65]—as documented in the studies numbered above. Can I put it any stronger? Shyness stinks. Don't let it ruin your life.

I suffered in high school from acute shyness, the kind that made me shake if I had to talk with a male. I just squeaked through college, forcing myself into activities that forced me to communicate with people. Realizing what my problem was, I started studying the well-liked students in terms of how they walked, how they talked, and how they responded to questions. I made lists of their personality traits and began reading about what I discovered was called "people skills" and "charisma." I studied the techniques of some of my more likeable professors and of people like Barbara Walters and those she interviewed. I analyzed every speaker I had the opportunity to hear, whether it was a film star accepting an Oscar or my clergyman communicating with his parishioners. I hungered for the ease with people that they seemed to have. I became conscious of my body language, my listening skills, and my voice. I worked on all of them, and, little by little, I found people responding in a warmer way to me. With all this self-analysis, I found it ironic that the less I thought about myself, and the more I genuinely cared about them, the more they were drawn to me.

The medley of skills needed for smooth and charismatic communication is a never-ending study. Every day, I continue to learn something new.

Why have I spent the time telling you this? Just to let you know that you can overcome shyness. If it's a mild case or if it only comes on around certain people, the best way to start is as I did—simply by forcing yourself into situations where you must communicate with people. America is a country of self-help. You can find books, seminars, and audiotapes on every aspect of self-improvement and gain from every book, tape, or seminar you expose yourself to.

It's probably no consolation to know that 10 million American adults regularly suffer from shyness intense enough to be classified as a disease called "social anxiety disorder."[66]

A Sure Cure for "Butterfly Belly" When Talking to Beautiful Babes

But if yours is just a case of butterflies when talking to attractive women, force yourself to talk to not only the "lookers" but also, to be politically correct, those who are, shall we say, "appearance-challenged." Talk to "weight-challenged," "old age-challenged", and all sorts of other non-contenders for your amorous pursuits. In fact, talking to strangers to develop a "chatty" public personality is one of the most effective ways of curing a case of specialized shyness.

Even the Best Generals Have a Fallback Position

With this sequence, you can be pretty sure of success. However, even the best of wartime generals have a fallback position. If she should make the foolish mistake of not recognizing your superior intelligence, wit, and savior faire, you should have such a fallback position that preserves your ego (and perhaps may make her change her mind).

Let's say you approach the lady sitting alone at the bar, you try to pick her up, and she says, "Sorry, I have a boyfriend." You can respond with "He's a lucky man."

If she says, "I'm not in the mood to talk now," you can respond with "That's my great loss."

If she makes it evident she doesn't welcome your approach, you can say, "Please consider it a compliment."

If she laughs in your face, you can simply tell her "You have a beautiful laugh."

If she moans, simply respond by saying, nicely, "I only make the most beautiful women ill."

If you are more comfortable with wit than with compliments, you can try something like this when she ignores you: "Whoops, I forgot. Let me go take off my invisible cloak; I'll return when you can see me." But be careful with jokes. Compliments work better.

Whether it turns her "No" into a "Well, on second thought" or a "Yes" is yet to be seen. But one thing is sure. As in leaping out of a window when you know the firemen are holding the net, you will find picking her up much easier if you have a foxy face saver or a respectfully funny line to fall back on.

27

Why All the B.S.?

You say you don't like the bar scene or having to go through the whole charade at a party? You think it's ridiculous to clock how long it takes for her to look up at you again so you'll know if she likes you? And you think it's silly to insist you approach from a certain angle and not turn toward her too fast?

Does all this sound too complicated? (Hey, I never promised you this was the 1040EZ form of sex.) Perhaps you'd prefer it to be a bit simpler, such as it is for Balinese men who ask a girl to have intercourse by simply pronouncing the name of her sex organ. (How far do you think you'd get with a lady in today's world by walking up to her on the street, pointing, smiling, and saying, "Beaver?") Sirino men are a tad more subtle. They can ask directly but must whisper their request.[67] (Believe me, no matter how softly you whisper, "Wanna get laid?" she's going to call the cops.)

It's not just on tropical islands and in faraway lands that such blatant approaches exist. Right here on our own soil, the Crow Indians of North America didn't have singles bars. When a man was interested in a woman, he would sneak up to her tent at night and slip one hand in. If he got lucky, his fingers found her genitals. He would play with them for a while, and, if she liked his handi-

193

work, she'd invite him to follow his hand and replace it with another bodily appendage.[68]

In the light of all this, I'd say parties and singles bars are pretty good bets. But please don't limit yourself to those venues. Women everywhere are looking for love. Women signal men awaiting flights in airports, dining in restaurants, shopping in department stores, reading in parks, sitting in theaters, viewing paintings in galleries, and walking their dogs on streets. They are more aggressive than ever before, and the really good news is that nowadays they're looking for love, hot sex, and lots of fun, not necessarily a wedding band.

In fact, some girls get downright goofy when it comes to men. They're looking for a few laughs and a good time. Such behavior is so indicative of a woman enjoying your company that we've promoted it to a sex signal.

UNDERCOVER SEX SIGNAL #24:

The Goofy Girl

This sex signal can be either nervous and uncontrollable or contrived and flirtatious. Here Sandy is expressing her glee in much the same way that a little girl does when being told of an impending trip to Disneyland. Many women, especially the younger ones, get almost out of control, giggling and doing silly things, when they're with a man who excites them. They don't allow themselves to laugh and do goofy things around men who don't turn them on.

28

Cyber Matchmaking Is a *Virtual* Blast

Remember when you were a little shaver playing spin the bottle? The bottle had to stop sometime, and, because everyone had agreed to the rules of the game, you knew that you werc going to score a sure kiss. Of course, there were no guarantees that the bottle was going to point to the girl you wanted. But the mystery and anticipation made it kinda fun.

That's sort of like what finding love online is like. Except, instead of seven women you can possibly "kiss," you've got 7,000 (and that's just in your part of the country!). When you go to one of the major dot-com matchmakers and play *click-a-chick*, you're gambling that you'll find a gorgeous date; the love of your life; a great one-night stand; a paranoid, demented, delusional (really screwed-up) dame, or a plain dog. Ditto when you throw a dart at the newspaper personals. (There are fewer women to respond to, but at least none of them is G.U.—geographically undesirable.)

Whether appearing online or in the newspaper, these chicks all have two things in common. They are all single (or at least they claim they are), and they are all searching. No more hearing, "I already have a boyfriend," "Uh, sorry, I'm married," or "I'm not ready for another relationship." At least not at first.

Online romancing is a shopper's paradise, sort of like a QVC of chicks. You just sit at home, and the "product" comes on the screen. No more worrying about getting dressed, picking her up, wining and dining her, and then deciding you don't dig her—or vice versa. Online, there's no driving her home, that awkward pause followed by the white lie, and "Uh, well, I'll call you."

Get dressed? Heck, what for? Online, you can get naked and e-talk to her. It's fun, it's safe, and she might even be up for a round of cybersex.

But the very best thing about starting a relationship online, or so the men in my seminars tell me, is that you feel very little rejection up front. Some chick you clicked on doesn't return your e-mail? Big deal. There are a dozen others. That's a far cry from approaching a woman at a party and being confronted with her superior "Get lost, twerp" expression.

How to Win the Women-Online Game

Each matchmaking site works a little differently; essentially, however, you post your "profile" for women to appraise and you better believe that this is what they'll do. They'll noodle over every word you wrote, enlarge your photo on their screens to count every budding hair of your five o'clock shadow, and try to figure out, between the lines, how much money you make. They'll also get their antennae out for the other three basic qualities a woman wants in a relationship, in essence, a man who is strong, financially secure, respected, and emotionally caring.

So what's a guy to do? Advertise "Strong, rich and respected SWM seeks SWF for romantic evenings walking by the lake"?

No, but you can say it between the lines. Allude to your healthy interest in building things to make the "He's *strong!*" bell go off in her head. *Respect* can be taken care of by your mentioning some community or charity work you've done. *Emotionally available* or caring? Anything romantic, such as long walks or close dancing, will do. And there are hundreds of ways to hint at your *money*. "Enjoys European vacations," "Loves yacht sailing"—you get the idea. Do not, I repeat do not, lie. It will only lead to disappointment (hers and therefore yours) later on. However, do not feel guilty exaggerating your good qualities just a tad. You can bet your credit-card tab that she is doing the same.

Be especially on the lookout for her use of words like "Rubenesque" and "mature." ("Rubenesque" means fat and "mature" means practically prehistoric.) And understand that a woman usually comes with surprises—such as, perhaps the six kids she neglected to mention or the $200-per-day drug habit she's trying to kick.

That aside, since we all have a few hidden skeletons in our closets, the main challenge of the personals or online dating is (trumpet blare please) THE MEETING!

You've seen a picture of her face. She looks good. She's seen yours. Obviously, you looked good to her as well—or she wouldn't have agreed to meet you. You splash on an extra fistful of aftershave. You've chosen a nice restaurant where she can feel safe. You walk in, and there stands a chubby, overanxious woman fidgeting with her purse. There is no escape now. She looks up and says, "Oh, are you . . . ?"

"And you must be . . . ," you say—your heart sinking as you wonder whether you should feign appendicitis or an epileptic fit.

That, sadly, seems to be the report from the field about online dating. Many sing its praises, but the most common refrain is "Yeah, I'm making contact with a lot of people, but the moment we meet, it all fizzles out."

Oh, sure, you hear the occasional success story of Dick and Jane who met on line and rode happily off into cyberspace together. But the stats are not encouraging. Match.com, one of the largest online dating services, said it has enrolled 5 million members in six years and boasts 1,100 marriages. Big deal, one in 2,270 or .045 percent. Your odds are better going to one of the female fantasy islands I will discuss next, or standing on your own street corner whistling at the girls going by.

So what are the missing ingredients in the personals and online dating? *The missing ingredients are what Undercover Sex Signals is all about*—body language, voice tone, and subliminal signals.

All of the following statistics and quotes about online dating are from the *New York Times*, one of America's most-respected news sources.[69]

A doctoral student researching online dating said, "Online romances create a false intimacy among couples. Text-based relationships are very deceptive. People know only the good stuff and none of the bad. The missing pieces are filled in based on hope, not on reality."

Another doctor, at Rensselaer, agrees. He says, "You get the sensitivity and thoughtfulness. You don't get the waistline, hairline, fidgets, twitches, and interruptions."

"Whereas if you meet spontaneously," he continues, "you build your impression from real data, not from an idealized basis."

A male dater reports, "It's a trap. Your imagination fills in the blanks with exactly what you want." And so does hers!

Some online dating services claim that online suitors are more forgiving of small flaws. But psychologists don't buy it. They say the kid-in-the-candy-store effect makes them more apt to bail out of a potentially promising relationship—because they ask themselves, "Is this the best I can get?" Let me click and search again, and see what I get.

The *New York Times* concludes that "romances that flourish in chat rooms and e-mail often wilt at the first face-to-face meeting." In big bold type, they report: *Nonverbal communication is often what counts in a relationship, something that gets lost in the e-mail."*

Would I sound flaunting or self-righteous about *Undercover Sex Signals* at this point to tell the *New York Times* researchers, "Hey, guys, that's what we've been telling you!"

> To put it in less erudite terms, picking up a chick that digs your style is probably preferable to spending countless hours (not to mention dollars) on dating your ass off based on on-line introductions.

So, where to go? Try these five top hot spots that appeal to women.

The Best Places to Meet a Woman: Her Five Fantasy Islands

Women are all hopeless romantics. One of the first questions the girls ask one another at teenage pillow parties or sophisticated charity balls is "Where did you meet him?" It's borderline slutiness to answer "a bar," and "the mall" is much too mundane. It's much better that you made the scene in one of her fantasy dream locales. Where do you have the best luck meeting a woman? Here are five top picks.

1. *Yoga class.* Here you'll be surrounded by limber ladies and you'll be the big, sensitive, stud duck in the pond. Don't worry that you won't be able to do the "downward facing dog" or understand what the big deal about "the tree pose" is. The supple sweeties will think it's cute and be very happy to help you. Still worried about your macho image? Just tell them it's to get in better shape for football with the guys at work.

2. *A cruise ship.* This one is a sure-fire sizzler. On your next vacation, don't go fishing with the boys. Go on a cruise to anywhere and go fishing for all the girls you want. Single women out-number single men by a ratio of 6-to-1, and you'll have your pick. Meeting her dream man on a cruise is in the back of every woman's mind.

3. *A local park.* A little closer to home is an all-time favorite with knowledgeable womanizers. In lieu of a live-in man, lots of single girls get a dog to keep them warm at night. If you have aspirations of taking the place of one of those dogs, get a mutt of your own—the hornier the better (the dog, that is, not you). Then head for the nearest park with your guaranteed, four-legged, pick-up device. Look around for dogs that have gorgeous dames at the end of their leashes. Fido does the rest. (Just practice apologizing profusely so it sounds like you're *really* sorry when Fido tries to shag her little shaggy dog.)

4. *A lecture or a meeting of volunteers.* "Oh, why can't I meet a man who shares my interest in _____" (fill in the blank). Whether it's opera, ballet, pre-Columbian artifacts, or South American reptiles, solo women flock to lectures. Even more women do charity work. A can't fail plan is to volunteer for a cause you believe in. (Not only will you meet the girls, you'll do some good in the world.)

5. *The nearest Victoria's Secret lingerie store.* This one is for the cool and the courageous only. Take a deep breath and put on your best, "I'm so embarrassed to be here" look or you risk coming off like a pervert who prefers making love to panties rather than to the person in them. Once you've got the expression down pat, it's time to work on your lines. Try to invoke something wholesome like your family.

"My sister's birthday is coming up, and she said she loves Victoria's Secret, uh, er, stuff. What would you recommend?" Or what about, "I wanted to get a fun gift for my Mother, and . . ." "Grandma?" (Hey, mine wears a garter-belt. But that's before they were considered sexy.)

One of Women's Most Misunderstood Signals

This brings us to the sex signal, which men often misinterpret as a woman being standoffish or snobbish. Women, who since they were little girls have been envying the glamorous models in the fashion magazines and trying to be just like them, have learned the art of the pose. The clever ones know their "best side" and instinctively turn it whenever there is a camera in sight. And clever women know what angle their bodies look most attractive in, so they flash it whenever an attractive man is in sight.

UNDERCOVER SEX SIGNAL #25:

The Pose

Here Ashley, very cognizant that her long slender lines will be accentuated by sitting at an angle and raising one leg over the other, will often take this position when she spots a man she likes. Every woman's body is different so each will strike a slightly different pose. But you can be assured that she will instinctively take a "pretty pose" when first spotting a man she wants to attract. A woman's body usually undulates a bit in their favorite position and it will most likely be blended with a little self-caressing. Don't mistake it for being standoffish. If she keeps her eyes on you more than three seconds or throws repeated glances your way you know the pose is for you.

Knowing that most men fall into the category of "breast man" or "leg man," another obvious pose that women often take is baring their legs. They are usually able to pull it off as though it were accidental. Sure, it's as accidental as putting cheese in the mousetrap, and it works better for man-trapping.

UNDERCOVER SEX SIGNAL #26:

The Leg Show

Here three women are using their legs big-time. Those are sophisticated Jade's legs on the right. She's twisting her black-knit stocking legs around each other at an enticing angle. Sensual Ashley in the center is again flashing a little thigh. (Can you see what other signal she's giving you with her right leg?) And Vivacious Sandy is swinging her left leg back and forth as if to say, "Hey, look at mine!"

The Turnabout
(Using My U.S.S.s to Turn Her On)

29

Your Biggest Sex Signal Is YOU!

Unlike the reverse, it wouldn't be a turn-on for you to run your middle finger around the rim of a glass while staring into her eyes, or suck seductively on a swizzle stick while letting your sandal dangle from your toes. Most women don't respond to blatantly sexual moves. There are, of course, certain of the basic signals that will work with her such as, subtly mirroring her movements while conversing or, depending on the degree of intimacy you've attained, touching her. However, the most important sex signal you have to convey is YOU—how you look, how you sound, how you move. Essentially, who you are (or aren't) is one big sex signal to her. I'm not going to kid you and say that any poorly dressed, bloated, old-bean-bag can work magic on a woman through using U.S.S.s (Although, everything in the book is true because, if a woman did have an old-bean-bag fetish and slung some sex signals at him, he would have a chance with her.)

Play by the Numbers to Get the Best You Can Get

Conversely, I'm going to say that the more refined, better dressed, and more intelligent looking you are, the better success you're going to have with women because more of them will turn themselves into sex signal sirens for you.

Tit-for-Tat Love?

There is a vast body of research called the "Equity Theory" of love that should be on the top of the required reading list for every man who is sincerely interested in women.[70] It shows, beyond any reasonable doubt, that women make their decision about a potential lover with all the reckoning they would in buying a house or a horse. (Men do too, but we're talking about women here.)

What is your legal tender that is negotiable for her in love? The researchers have reduced it to six basic qualities. The higher you rate on the six-point scale, the "better" woman you can get. Before continuing to read, give some thought to what six points you would be looking for in the woman of your dreams, the woman you'd want to have for keeps. Be honest now . . . no woman can read your mind (although many think they can).

Following are six questions about what you are looking for in a partner. These are the same questions a woman asks herself about a man when considering him as a possible match. Some of the questions are worded with qualities that are not necessarily a combo. Do the best you can; answering whatever comes to your mind first.

1. How important is her physical appearance?

2. How important is her wealth? That can be money, property, or even earning capacity.

3. How important is it that she has status and prestige in whatever group you choose to focus on? Professional? Church? Circle of friends?

4. How important is her intelligence, knowledge, or education?

5. How important is it that she has smooth social graces and
   a good personality?

6. How important is her character or inner nature?

At this point, you might be saying, "Hey, who's talking about
the long run. What about tonight?"

We spoke earlier about the vast divergence in the way the male
and the female of our complex species think. One of the contrapo-
sitions concerns "the one night stand." Unlike you, a woman mea-
sures a man with whom she might consider a short fling with the
same ruler she holds up for a possible husband. Thus, the higher
you rate in the Big Six above, the closer you are to a roll in her hay.

Curious about how your answers compared with other folks
seeking love and romance? I often ask participants in my seminars
to secretly write on a card how critical each of these qualities is in
a potential love partner, and then sign their cards with only "M"
for male, and "F" for female. I've chosen a selection of answers from
men and women that were most representative.

1. How important is Physical Appearance?

   MEN: "Very important," "Unless she had good qualities
   too, I'd get immune to her good looks," "I always feel
   proud taking out a good-looking woman," "Damn important. I'd be a liar to say otherwise."

   WOMEN: "Not that important," "Not important that he
   be 'typically' good looking, but I like character in a man's
   face," "Not that important but I do like him to have a good
   body."

2: How important are Possessions or Money?

   MEN: "Not at all," "Hey, it's cool if she has money, but
   it doesn't make any big difference," "Well, I'd be a little
   put off if she started asking me for money early in the

relationship, but how much money she earns isn't crucial."

WOMEN: "I certainly wouldn't marry a man just for his money, but I like him to earn more than me," "It's becoming less important now that I'm earning more, but I guess I'm still a little old-fashioned," "Sure it's important."

3. How important are Status and Prestige?

MEN: "It's not important," "Never really thought about it that much," "I wouldn't want her to have a bad reputation, but she doesn't have to have a lot of status."

WOMEN: "Depends on how you define status—I like people to respect him," "If he's a good man, he'll automatically have that, no?" "I am attracted to power."

4. How important are intelligence and knowledge?

MEN: "I like a woman to be bright," "I hate stupid women," "I want my woman to be smart, but maybe not quite as smart as me," "I like her to be intelligent but not go around showing it off."

WOMEN: "Very important," "Intelligence is a big factor for me," "Education is not all that important but I like him to have 'street smarts,'" "I want to know he's smart enough to take care of his family," "I have my masters' degree so I suppose I'd like him to at least have that."

5. How important are Social Graces and Personality?

MEN: "Yes, I like a girl with a great personality—that and looks are the two most important things to me," "I want her to be fun to be with," "Sure, I don't want her to embarrass us at social functions," "I'm a businessman and I'd like my wife to be able to entertain smoothly."

WOMEN: "He doesn't need to be a laugh a minute, but

I like a guy with a good personality," "Social Graces are important to me—I'm sick of guys who don't know what fork to use," "Personality is extremely important."

6. How important are Character or Inner Nature?
   MEN: "Very important."
   WOMEN: "Very, very important," "It's probably the most important thing."

So there it is, straight from the source's mouth. This six-category scale alone, however, has its fallacies because the words have different connotations to different people. It also doesn't take into consideration other important variables like religion, age, how many children they want, how their family feels about the partner, and what their definition of a relationship is.

That aside (and that's a pretty hefty "aside"), what fascinated me was the accuracy with which Equity theorists were able to predict whether two people would be happy together based on what they bring to the table.

Test to See If You and She Will Be a Happy Couple

Have a particular lady in mind? If you want to determine what chances Equity theorists would predict that you and a chosen partner, have for riding happily off into the sunset together, take this quiz. (But keep your tongue firmly implanted in your cheek throughout.)

On the "Bo Derek" scale of one to ten (10 being tops, 1 being zip), rate yourself, and the partner of your choice.

	Partner	Me
1. Physical Appearance		
2. Possessions or Money		
3. Status or Prestige		
4. Information or Knowledge		
5. Social Graces or Personality		
6. Inner Nature		
	Partner's total	My Total

Finished? Now add up all of your partner's (or desired partner's) scores. Put his or her total at the bottom. Then add all of your scores and put the total on the bottom. Last step, subtract the smaller number from the larger. What is the difference?

Difference in the Two Numbers: _____

If it is 5 or above, the theorists say the relationship probably wouldn't work. (The higher scoring partner would get bored or take advantage of the relationship. The lower number would always feel he or she didn't measure up.) Four is borderline. Three is OK. Two and one are great. Zero? You've hit pay dirt. Don't mess that one up. She's a "Keeper."

30

How to Raise Your Score with Women

Remember back in high school when your buddy fixed you up on a blind date and you asked about her looks? He patted you on the back and said, "Oh, she's got a great personality!" That was the tip-off that you should bring her a flea collar rather than a corsage.

But really, what about your looks? Women say looks are not that important. But will a fat wallet make up for a fat gut? Will a strong personality make up for weak biceps? Will lots of creativity make up for little hair?

Let's just say that it's lucky for you good looks are not as important as personality to a woman. You can change the latter, but Mother Nature doesn't like you messing around too much with the former. Yet looks are more important to a woman than to a man. Sound like contradictory statements? They're not. Let me explain.

Objective good looks are higher on the male wish list. Most guys fancy a long-legged filly with big knockers and a tiny waist. But line up 100 young women along a wall and ask you, the living peter meter, how many you are attracted to. You'd probably find about half of them that you wouldn't kick out of bed.

Now, line up a hundred guys and this time it's ladies choice. The results? Even though most of the guys in the lineup are relatively good-looking studs, only a few of them would really ring her bell. Why? Because a woman is far more *specific* in what she is looking for. If she wants a man with character, your face must show character for her to be instantly physically attracted to you. If she values a sense of humor, you'd better have some credible laugh lines. If intelligence is her big turn-on, your chrome-dome better shine.

Any generalizations? Sure. Here is what the *British Journal of Social Clinical Psychology* found that most women liked in a man's face:

> *Women are attracted to men whose appearances elicit their nurturing feelings; who appear to possess sexual maturity and dominance characteristics; who seem sociable, approachable and of high social status.*
>
> *Individuals who display an optimal combination of neotenous (boyish) features of large eyes, the mature features of prominent cheekbones and a large chin, the expressive feature of a big smile, and high-status clothing were seen as more attractive than other men.*[71]

Now, let's try some plain English. That's saying, women like a man with strong features, who looks like he would be a good and caring provider. But she also likes a touch of boyishness so she could mother him. Mother Nature strikes again.

Boys blessed with full, rich manes of shiny hair may find this next question meaningless. But many of your less hirsute brothers want to know how women feel about their bald or balding heads.

If you're one of the growing number of men in our aging population who furtively holds a mirror up to the back of their heads for a weekly inspection of how many hairs they've recently said "Happy landing" to—and wonder if it's time to run out and buy some Grecian formula—read on. You will love science's answer. (Maybe if you're jobhunting instead of dame hunting, you won't.)

In a study called "Impression Formation as a Function of Male Baldness" (or more simply "What do people think of baldies?") researchers used a computer morphing procedure to produce full cranial hair for a naturally bald thirtyish man.[72] They then showed his photo to everybody and anybody who would look at it and asked them to answer a few questions.

Tallying the results, the guy with the full mane was rated "significantly more dominant, dynamic, and masculine" than his baldie brother. He was also perceived as younger. But, now here's the good news for horny baldies the world over, and I quote the abstract, "There was no difference in mean ratings of attractiveness between the photographs" according to the women surveyed.

A final hairy word to the wise. If they're gone, they're gone. Do not, I repeat, *do not*, save a few long hairs to comb over the top of your head. Everybody sees your chrome dome shining through, and you must live in fear of windy days.

Even worse are toupees. She may enjoy running her fingers through your hair. But she doesn't want to keep it.

"So what about hair plugs," you ask. No woman would enjoy caressing a head that felt like coarse[36] grade sandpaper.

Women Judge My Hairstyle? You've Got to Be Kidding!

Gentlemen, I kid you not. Nothing escapes a woman's scrutiny about you. Paying as much attention to detail as a Broadway producer casting a million dollar show, she scrutinizes you tip to toe. Every detail from your hairstyle to the shine on your shoes is, in a way, a sex signal she uses to judge whether she wants to invest an evening with you.

There's obviously no "right" or "wrong" hairstyle but, since the subject of men's hairstyles showed up a number of times on the blue cards in my seminar, we took a poll. Here's what women in one class said about the various styles:

Precisely cut, blow dried, sprayed: You might look in the mirror in the morning and say, "That's part of my power image," but women actually don't like it. If a man has a too neatly coifed head, she's thinking, "This dude is vain and has a bloated self image."

Dyed hair: Fine if it's a really good job and she doesn't notice it.

Long hair: "What about long hair?" many men ask me. They think it makes them look more creative and artistic. That it could do. But unless you're an artist, musician or rock star with a recognizable name, a woman probably thinks you don't earn much money.

There was a guy with short hair in front, and a ponytail in back. He asked for the women's comments and told them that he felt that he could fit in with both the long hairs for playing, and the conservative world for work. But the women didn't buy it. They were ruthless. They said that his style means he's probably "not in the big leagues" and he "cares too much about fitting in with his long hair buddies."

Do you detect a theme emerging here? Women do not like any style on a man that echoes insecurity or the opposite, pomposity.

The best, woman-pleasing, style that 9.9 out of 10 women prefer is a professional, neat, clean, un-styled, un-dyed, and un-sprayed head of hair. That says, "I'm not cheap, overly vain, or overly concerned with any one group's opinion of me. I'm successful and I care about my grooming."

What About My Abs and Pecs? Height?

Pull out the tape measure because we're going to hit below the belt. Average build is in, but the gals like you to be bigger above the waist than below. The studies tell us, the ladies prefer "V's" to "pears."[73] But that's a matter of class too. Women who were born with a cheap plastic spoon in their mouths generally prefer muscle men. Conversely, highly paid professional women, find hefty beefcake downright distasteful. It's the slim and sensitive body types for them.

What about height? Let's look at some statistics. Practically every president who got the popular vote (that doesn't mean elected these days,) in the United States since 1900 was the taller of the two candidates. And, according to the *Wall Street Journal*, taller graduating college students (6'2" and over) receive an average starting salary 12.4 percent higher than those who were under 6 feet tall. One would assume therefore, that when it comes to love and sex, women prefer tall men.

Well, there's good news for guys who come in under the 6 ft pole. Apparently, when fantasizing about the guy in the horizontal position, taller wasn't better. Women of all sizes—short, medium and tall—rated a variety of men on their sexual attractiveness. The medium-sizers won.

So, if you're not a tall V-shaped gentleman with just a touch of beefcake, is it hopeless? Not at all. If you'd like to get a few more women whispering "he's soo handsome" when you pass, remember to become a "good mover." If you want to up your ante in the looks department, study the body positions of the guys in the ads for Calvin Klein briefs or Armani jackets. You know, the ones with that intense "I can see right through your dress" look in their eyes, and just enough five o'clock shadow to certify their manliness. The really cool part is the way they're standing, weight on one foot, jacket held by two fingers and casually thrown over one shoulder, head cocked at just the right angle. In the modeling business they're called "good movers." And you can do it too.

You don't need to go around posing all over the place or you'll look like just that, a posy. But do start paying attention to how you *move*. Strong masculine movements are in. (Have a good stride.) Courteous movements are in. (Stand up when she comes back from the restroom to the restaurant table.) Protective movements are in.

(Offer the lady your arm when you cross the street.) Loving movements are in. (Straighten her collar or adjust her hair after putting her coat on.) Cool moves are in!

Does She Really Care What I Wear?

In a word, "YES!" It would blow your mind to know what a woman notices about you. When you wear expensive or well-coordinated clothes, it subconsciously signals to her your ability to provide for her offspring. Don't blame the lass. Once again, she's just doing what Mother (Nature) told her to. Even the waitress from the "One Horse Coffee Shop" (who has never been outside of the town it's named after) has an uncanny sense of how much things cost—must be in their genes!

Before scouring the studies for any mention of civies, I committed the sin of projecting. As a woman, I adore designer duds and would shop 'till I dropped for elegant outfits to knock my date's socks off. What a waste of money! The evidence was open and shut. Since a man is going to mentally undress a woman anyway, why spend hard earned cash on clothing with some fancy signature on the label? *Not so the other way around.*

> Just because you don't give a flying fig about what's on your back doesn't mean she doesn't. Unlike you, she does not have a naked imagination. She is not going to mentally undress you and imagine your bulging biceps and wonderful washboard abs beneath. Your clothes count with her!

The proof of this little tidbit was a study conducted at Syracuse University. Both men and women were shown photographs of opposite sex individuals.[74] The women ranged from fabulous foxes all the way down to dumpy dogs. But here's the rub. Some of the dogs were exquisitely dressed and some of the foxes wore frumpy frocks. I've got to hand it to you guys. You weren't fooled one bit. You saw right through the expensive duds and picked out which ones were dogs in fox's clothing and vice versa.

The women weren't so sharp. (Hmm, or were they? Depends on what they're looking for.) The men ranged from Kevin Costner class destroyers down to pictures of guys even the photographer would be afraid to be alone with in the darkroom. Likewise they were dressed from top of the line designer duds to cheap bargain basement rags.

While viewing the photos, the women were asked six questions such as "Who would you choose to marry?" and "Which man would you like a date with," down to a rather surprising query (considering it was from a respected university study), "Who would you choose for a one time only roll in the hay?"

Turns out that how the male was dressed was *extremely* important to the women. The better dressed a man was, the higher marks he received in all six categories—including, "one night nookie."

Alas, in spite of millions of years of sexual evolution, men and women still approach romance differently. Gentlemen, even when slumming it with the intention of picking up a one-night stand, don't go out dressed like an unmade bed. And even though you've got great buns and think you're a killer in those Levi's that look like they were put on with a spray can, you'll score much better at a pick-up bar in a pair of tailored Brooks Brothers slacks. That doesn't mean you can't be casual. But be casual chic, not casual cheap. Here are a few lady pleasing hints: The temperature's skyrocketing and you want to wear a short-sleeved shirt? Don't. It short-circuits your sex appeal. Wear, rather, a long-sleeved shirt with the sleeves rolled up.

Socks? No matter how casual, socks should match the tone and color of your trousers. And never let that yukky bit of hairy leg show between the sock and the pants when seated. The no sock look? Some guys think it's cool but it's really just stinky. Wearing a belt? It should match your shoes, both color and finish (matte or shiny).

Shoes? Even if she's not conscious of it, women were born with X-ray vision to spot a pair of posh-foot pinchers halfway across a crowded ballroom.

One of my actress friends, named Christiana, was a confessed and unabashed social climber. She once got us invited to a posh sit down dinner party of six men and six women.

After the party, riding home on the subway because we couldn't afford a cab, Christiana said to me above the rumble of the train, "Clifford asked me out. He's taking me to see *The Fantastiks*. I told him I've never seen it although I'd auditioned for it."

"Which one was Clifford?" I asked.

"The tall one with the Bruno Magli's."

"The what?"

"Shoes," she shouted. "The Bruno Magli shoes."

Considering we were sitting down the major part of the evening and couldn't see under the table, I asked how she happened to notice his shoes.

"How can you *not* notice?" she asked, exasperated at my obtuse powers of perception.

"Oh, come on, what were the others wearing?" I challenged her.

Christina proceeded to announce the role call of men's footwear. "Kyle had on a pair of Ferragamo wingtips, Andre was wearing Wallabees, Bill was in Charles Jordan loafers."

"And John?" I asked.

"Oh, Kilties," she said disparagingly as though he'd been wearing paratrooper boots. She won.

Gentlemen, I am *not* saying all women are as fanatic about your shoes as Christiana but, sloppy clodhoppers will make a much worse impression on her than on any of your buddies who wouldn't notice anything on your feet short of 4-inch stiletto heels.

Jacket? Above all, expensive soft lush fabrics. Women are into touch, remember? Most importantly, make sure your clothes drape beautifully on your body if you want her to do the same.

> Your best bet is to take a woman shopping with you; your sister or an ex-girlfriend (not an embittered one) will do nicely. Even better—are you sitting down?—hire an image consultant to do what they call a "closet analysis" for you. Do you think image consultants are only for super stars and residents of Easy Street? Think again. They're for guys, smart ones at least.

Put out the word and you'll probably find a young and talented image consultant whose fee for an analysis is in the double digits. I did.

I met Julia working at a SoHo art gallery. Turns out she moonlights in the evening as an image consultant. Granted, the idea of having an image consultant was just too "la de da" for me. But, it turns out it was one of the smartest calls I ever made.

I then did a little arm-twisting on a male friend of mine, Phil. Phil was pretty savvy to undercover sex signals so he was successful with women—up to a point. He didn't understand why sometimes especially upscale women would turn him down. Little did he realize it was the way he dressed.

"Try it you'll love it," I told him. I dialed Julia's number and dragged him kicking and screaming to the phone. As it was ringing, he put his hand over his mouth refusing to speak.

"I'll never cook a meal for you again," I threatened. That didn't do it.

"I'll never introduce you to any babes again!" I added.

"Uh, hello, Julia?" he said. "I'm a friend of Leil's and . . . "

Julia came over the next evening and did a complete "closet analysis" for Phil. Throughout the evening it was a cacophony of

"Keep this."

"Trash that."

"Keep this."

"Oh, Gawd, *never* wear that!"

"Ooh, this is terrific."

"And this is *you*."

"Don't be caught dead in that."

"This goes with that."

"That is great with this."

"Now this will work beautifully if you just add these pants."

When it was all over and Julia left, Phil collapsed on the couch piled high with clothes. I calculated for him how much money he had saved. I told him, "On the double digit fee you paid Julia, you'll probably never have to buy any clothes again—just take good care of the ones you have."

He moaned. I could tell that some less evolved giblet inside him was making him think back to decades ago when his mother said, "Phil, go change your shirt. You look like a bum!" I asked him if he enjoyed it. He answered, "How could I ever have continued on with life not knowing gray and black are 'me?' And browns and beige are sudden death? Even my best friend wouldn't tell me that, for casual wear, reds are 'the ultimate awesome,' but if there's any blue in it, girls will mistake me for a corpse?"

"Cut the rap, Phil. You know you benefited." I interpreted his groan as a sure sign that he was happy. At least I'm sure the Salvation Army was the next day when they came to pick up three bags of clothes that, Julia commanded him, "Don't get caught *dead* in!"

I could go on ad infinitum. But I'll spare you and simply say: *Make sure your packaging—from their first sight of you right on down to your smell—is carefully calibrated to attract the kind of gal you want*. And, unless you're an expert in not only fashion, but also human nature and what others find appropriate and attractive, let a pro do the job for you.

Still going to do it on your own are you? Well, I can't threaten you as I did Phil. At least take a look at the best book I've found on the subject. It's called *Casual Power* by Sherry Maysonave. And, unless you're one of those dudes who insists on wearing backward baseball caps and baggy jeans with the crotch skimming your knees, it will stand you in good stead.

Incidentally, at one turning point in your life I'm sure you had to make the great skivvies decision: Boxers or briefs? Brief briefs or full briefs? Plain boxers or bright boxers with kaleidoscopic patterns of tippling glow-in-the-dark *Playboy* bunnies?

> In spite of millions of years of sexual evolution, men and women still approach romance differently. Even when tom-catting for a one-night stand, do not go out dressed like an unmade bed. Dress as though you were auditioning to be her husband.

The result of the Official Dr. Lowndes Seminar Participants Survey says women prefer good quality (clean!) briefs on a man. But not *too* brief. Unless you're Brad Pitt, that is. But I digress.

Oh, and one last hint. Do not spray cologne on your privates for a first date. The whiff coming from the south exposes that you expect some southern exposure too early on.

Beware! Your Home Has Hundreds of Land Mines

Sooner or later, the little lady is going to want to see one of your biggest sex symbols. (No, not that one.) It's your home. For her, it's not a visit to your pad; it's a reconnaissance mission. Nothing will escape her eagle eyes. If she finds one negative thing, it can blow the entire relationship.

You scramble around and throw all your dirty shirts on the floor of the closet, tell your scrungy socks to go run under the bed, and you try to figure how that vacuum cleaner your mother gave you two birthdays ago works.

Your date arrives and, while you're going into the kitchen to get a couple of glasses of wine, coke, or beer for the two of you, she'll be sniffing around like the drug addicted German Shepherds at the airport for clues to your personality.

At some point she'll probably want to use the bathroom. You can be sure she'll peek into your medicine cabinet. What will she find? Will ten packs of condoms fall out? A cascade of valium? Your other girlfriend's lip gloss and nail polish? I suggest you take inventory of everything in your medicine chest, your dresser, and under your bed and stash it at the bottom of your closet. And, if she's going to be spending any time alone at your place, bury it in the backyard.

Once I had to walk through a date's bedroom to get to the only bathroom in the house. He'd just been giving me this heartfelt line about how he hadn't had intimate relations with a woman in over two years. I glanced at his bed table and saw a pair of false eyelashes sticking to the side of it. (Obviously just peeled off in the dark and placed there in the past night or two since the glue doesn't hold very long.)

Everything is a clue to your nature—even the type of toilet paper in your bathroom! Do you go for the more expensive soft plushy kind, or do you go for the cheapie kind, so scratchy it feels like newspaper?

The Second She Enters Your Office, She's Sherlock Holmes

Your office artifacts get the same scrutiny. Like what photos do you have around your desk?

Your kids?

"Well, he did tell me about them," she's thinking. *"But are they getting all his money in child support?"*

A photo of your kids and ex-wife?

"Uh oh, I smell trouble here."

An ex-girlfriend?

Bigger trouble. "Is she really an 'ex'?"

Politicians or celebrities?

"I better get a closer look to make sure he's in the picture too, or it's really strange."

Be careful what calendar you have on the wall. That's a real litmus test for the little lady. Is it a Sierra Club calendar, an Arthur Anderson for our valued clients calendar, or a nude pinups calendar.

Forget about the fact that you had nothing to do with it and your office was decorated by the fruitcake they hired to do the whole firm. She'll still analyze how your space is laid out.

Is your desk forming a barrier between yourself and any visitors?

"Is he insecure or does he think that it's a status symbol?"

Is your space more open?

"Ah, he's more egalitarian."

Are the guest chairs as comfortable as yours?

"And he cares about people."

It's not just the artifacts and layout she makes note of. She'll be judging everybody's reaction and respect for you even as you walk past the cubicles.

Do they smile, wave, and say "Hi"?

Do they instantly try to look busy?

Do they avoid looking at him?

Do they roll their eyes or say "humph" as if to say, "There he is showing off another woman"?

Brains Win over Brawn, Every Time

For those of you who feel The Man Upstairs shortchanged you in the looks department, never fear. That doesn't mean you're going to be shortchanged in the dame department. Let me tell you about one of the littlest guys I know who is also one of the biggest winners with women. My friend Jeff has a big butt and fortunately the brains to match. He and I were having lunch a couple of years ago when he told me that he, and about 20 other guys, had been asked to participate in the Cancer Society's Bid for Bachelors. He told me some of the other guys were pretty cool competition—a few football players, local celebrities, and an assortment of certified hunks.

I knew that Jeff wanted at least some bids for two reasons. One, he believed deeply in the cause, and the amounts the women bid went to charity. And two, he didn't want the humiliation of being the guy who got the least bids.

When I heard that he couldn't even talk to the female bidders, that all they could do is see his picture and read a description of the "dream date" he would take them on, I didn't hold out much hope for him.

A couple of months went by and I didn't talk with Jeff. I ran into him at a speakers convention and didn't want to ask about what I was sure had turned out to be a mortifying experience. However, curiosity finally got the better of me. "Hey Jeff, how did you do in that Cancer Society Bid for Bachelors thing?"

Now, given Jeff's height, 5'5", and similar butt radius, what "dream date" would you devise to encourage some of the women to bid for you? (Remember, you have to pay for the date.)

Jeff answered, "Well, I was up against some pretty stiff competition, so I decided to use a basic marketing technique of carving off a 'market niche.' From past personal experience it seemed like about a third of the women I had dated over the years had cats.

And those who had cats were fanatical about them. So I created a date package geared specifically to 'Cat Lovers.'

"First my date and I would be picked up by a chauffeur driven Cat-o-lac to be taken to the Columbus Zoo. There, in the Lion's Pavilion, surrounded by exotic cats from around the world, we would have a candlelight dinner for two catered by a local restaurant called Katzingers. The centerpiece would be composed mainly of cattails and pussy willows.

The limo would take us to the stage show *Cats*. On the way we would listen to music on tape from Cat Stevens, and she would keep the tape as a memento of the evening. And just in case the evening would be too much, I advertised that I had Dr. Myron Katz on standby at Grant Memorial to perform complimentary catscans. It was a cat lovers date come true."

A little more optimistic about the answer I'd get this time, I asked, "So how did you do?"

"I brought in the second largest bid for the evening. Mike Tommzak, quarterback for the Chicago Bears, came in first."

When it comes to women, creativity, humor, and brains win out over brawn every time—even if there's additional big butt liability.

A lot of guys find love online, or through the personals and dating services these days. Unfortunately, most of them are in the dark ages thinking that success and money are what turns a woman on. They write their ads as though life were fundamentally tragic.

Well, women won't hold it against you if you've got more money than you can wash. In fact, we'll even help you launder it. But telling us about the size of your wad, or your rod, isn't going to impress us. It's better to remember the funny thing that happened on the way to the forum: "Make 'em laugh, make 'em laugh, make 'em laugh!"

Remember the most gorgeous toon ever drawn, Jessica? When asked, "Why do you love that funny looking little Roger Rabbit?"

She swiveled her incredibly awesome hips and crooned a breathy, "He makes me laugh."

How to Be a Man of Mystery

Most women adore a man they can't figure out. That's part of the bad-boy allure. But here's how you can be a good guy and still have that air of mystery about you. As you now know, it doesn't matter whether you are the Big Wig who owns controlling interest in all of creation or you work in the mailroom at Macy's, women love fine looking threads on you. Instead of your next "buy five and get one free" K-Mart shirts, save up and buy one designer dud from St. Laurent, Mason, Dolce e Gabbana, or Versace. You just invested in season tickets to see your team play ball and can't justify the expense for the threads? Go to the Salvation Army store, close your eyes, and run your hand down the shirt rack. Grab the first thing your hand reaches that feels as soft as a mouse and you've hit paydirt.

Wrong size? OK, OK, at least spend the three bucks, cut the designer label out and sew it into your favorite K-Mart shirt. (But then it will only fool the woman you're on undressing terms with already—*maybe*.)

Especially if you're "just a regular guy," buy one or more of the following. When she notices and asks about it, just toss it off with that "Oh, this old thing?" attitude and simply say, "I liked it so I bought it." Then let the subject drop. Cool!

A designer pen (Cartier, Mt. Blanc, Aurora or any writing instrument with a foreign name on it will do. Bic just doesn't cut it with women)

A money clip, especially monogrammed

Leather slippers, no old fuzzies with holes in them

A monogrammed handkerchief or shirt

Bonus: the edge of a platinum or gold laminated card peeking out of your wallet. (She'll assume it's an expensivo exclusivo American Express or Carte Blanche for high rollers only.)

Your U.S.S. Certification

31

Are You a Certified
U.S.S. Man Yet?

I have a good buddy in Texas, named Dale, who says, "Ya gotta be book-learned and hog smart to get what you want in this world."

Well, by now, you are definitely "book-learned" in undercover sex signals. You can tell better than 99.999 percent of the male population if a woman likes you or not. You can now walk into a bar, a party, a meeting, or a gym and with one sweep of your eyes know which women's bodies are saying, "Yes, c'mon over here, Big Boy" and which are saying, "No, don't bother me." Like knowing how to use the alphabet's 26 letters, you have her 26 signals to piece together her whole script concerning *you*.

You are now, essentially, a sexual polygraph machine. Your new skill in reading women lets you know which chicks you'll have success with and which ones might blow you off. You can be assured that if you concentrate on only the "yes" crowd, no woman will ever again rebuff your advances.

Now comes the "hog smart" part. That means, before you start fantasizing about picking up Jennifer Lopez or Britney Spears, that you understand the score. *You must make the move only on women who you know are receptive to you.* But knowing that should be no problem for you now.

Many of the men's books on my now overloaded and sagging bookshelves promised much and delivered little. They promised that you could get *any* woman if you just did what they said. Get real! Everything in *Undercover Sex Signals* is. You now know the bottom line on how to tell if you have a chance with a woman before making any embarrassing blunders or, worse, getting rebuffed. *Undercover Sex Signals* holds no punches. It tells it like it is. And this knowledge will help you date increasingly more beautiful or accomplished women. It will give you the courage to make the approach when you spot the one woman who you know is right for you.

A Quick Review

"Oh, oh, back to book learning," I heard you thinking. Well, for just a moment. A final once-over is important. What I highly suggest is this: Visualize each of the signals. Picture walking into a room and seeing women giving you the eye while playing with their hair, tugging on their jewelry, or primping to lure you over.

Do you think visualization is psychological mumbo-jumbo? Think again! All professional and Olympic athletes do it. It doesn't matter what their sport is—divers, runners, jumpers, javelin throwers, lugers, swimmers, skaters, and acrobats—visualize being at their peak performance. If they didn't, they'd never achieve success.

I have a friend, Richard, who runs marathons. Once, several years ago, just three weeks before the big New York marathon, an out-of-control car crashed into Richard's and he was taken to the hospital. He was not badly injured. Nevertheless, his friends were sorry for him because, they figured, being laid up two weeks in bed would, naturally, knock him out of the beloved marathon.

What a surprise it was to them when, on that crisp November marathon morning in Central Park, there was Richard—all ready to run.

"Hey dude, are you nuts?" one of our friends called out. "You're in no shape to run. You've been in bed these past few weeks!"

"My body may have been in bed," he replied, "but I've been running."

"Huh?" we asked in unison.

"Yeah, every day. I ran that 26 miles, 385 yards, right there on my mattress." He said that, in his imagination, he saw the sights, heard the sounds, and felt the twitching movements in his muscles. He visualized himself racing in the marathon.

Richard didn't do as well as he had the year before, but it was a miracle that he finished the marathon—without injury and without excessive fatigue. It was all due to visualization. Visualization works in just about any endeavor you apply it to—including picking up on women's sex signals.

Try visualizing each of the following signals as they are mentioned. If you don't "see" it in your mind's eye, go back and reread about that particular undercover sex signal.

It Starts Real Early

We learned that chicks' little tricks go all the way back to the time they were still in the crib and, let's say, Daddy gave a big smile whenever they played peekaboo (#2). A few years later, sitting on her daddy's lap, she bats her pretty little eyelashes, sits up real pretty (#20), and says, "Oh Daddykins, I would just wuv to go to McDonald's and then go for ice cream afterwards." Gentlemen, those of you who have been dads will know I speak the truth when I say hardly any father can resist looking into her sweet innocent eyes and telling her "yes" because "turning her down would break her little heart." Thus, even at a very early age she was learning to control men by her body language.

By the time she is a teenager, she discovers that men will come over to meet her if she glances at them in the school cafeteria out of the corner of her eyes (#4). She sees how some guys break out into a sweat if she stands a little too close to them (#8) or if she caresses her own body while maintaining eye contact (#18). The guys think it is sexy to watch her put on lipstick (#16), run her fingers through her hair (#17), twist her necklace sensuously around her fingers (#5), or reveal her neck by lifting her hair (#13). It becomes obvious to her that men get turned on when she scrunches up her shoulders in pleasure (#19). Sometimes acting cute and goofy (#24) or even giggling with a girlfriend has, she discovers, the power to taunt a man (#1). She learns that a man finds it fetching when, like a shy geisha (#3), she looks away, only to look at him again. And she learns that men are more apt to approach her when, although it is an awkward position, she turns a "come-hither palm" (#12) toward them.

Young girls enjoy their newfound sexual power over men and begin to exploit it. As adults, they learn the drawing power of posing to show off their best angle (#25) or dangling a shoe in an enticing manner (#7). Men love it, they discover, when they expose a little bit of extra chest (#6), move their legs sensuously (#26), or raise an arm so they can see their usually hidden underarms (#14). When chatting with a man, they see how he responds when they move an object or a hand into his personal space (#9), subtly copy his movements (#21), lean toward him (#11), or "innocently" touch him (#10).

She uses the new signals, but she certainly doesn't forget the old ones. She still flutters her eyelashes and initiates games of peekaboo. Now, however, the stakes are higher. It's no longer McDonald's. It's Chez Expensive. And it's no longer candy; it's expensive jewelry and other gifts.

Pulling Out All the Stops

Women have also made one disturbing discovery, one they didn't bank on. They realized that many times they could be signaling their little hearts out and the guys just didn't get it. No matter how many times they ran their fingers through their hair or smiled at a man, he seemed oblivious.

At that point, do women give up? Many do. But the smart confident ones resort to more potent signals, such as licking their lips (#15), suggestively running a finger around a wine glass (#23), or sucking on a swizzle stick (#22). Smart girls!

And smart guy if he picks up on it. Remember, only one out of every 31 men does. And now you are in that tiny throng of men who know the score just by looking at a woman.

32

And Now for the Final U.S.S. Test

So, guys, are you ready for that quiz I warned you about at the beginning of *Undercover Sex Signals*? If you've read the book carefully, you should be able to ace it, no sweat. Don't worry about which number the sex signal is. *Just remember what she does and what it means!* For example, one of the answers to number one below is *The Perk-Up*, which happens to be Sex Signal #20. However, all you would need to write is something like: "The Perk-Up: When she sees me, she perks up, throwing her shoulders back and pushing her breasts out."

Or maybe, for some unknown reason, you just can't get the image of a certain signal out of your mind. Like, why in the world would you remember that shot of Tanya with a swizzle stick in her mouth? Hmm. Anyway, just look over the questions below and put it where it's most appropriate. You get the idea.

1. **Name the two instinctive signals a woman who is attracted to you will do when you first walk into a room.**
    Undercover Sex Signal: _____
    Undercover Sex Signal: _____

2. Name the one signal that two, or more, girls talking together will give if they like you.
Undercover Sex Signal: _____

3. Name three ways a woman across the room signals primarily with her eyes that she wants you:
Undercover Sex Signal: _____
Undercover Sex Signal: _____
Undercover Sex Signal: _____

4. Name the four signals that involve a woman's baring more skin to you to let you know that you turn her on.
Undercover Sex Signal: _____
Undercover Sex Signal: _____
Undercover Sex Signal: _____
Undercover Sex Signal: _____

5. Name the four signals that a woman sitting with you will throw to let you know she'd like more intimacy with you.
Undercover Sex Signal: _____
Undercover Sex Signal: _____
Undercover Sex Signal: _____
Undercover Sex Signal: _____

6. Name the six signals a woman gives with her hands that say, "You excite me."
Undercover Sex Signal: _____
Undercover Sex Signal: _____
Undercover Sex Signal: _____
Undercover Sex Signal: _____
Undercover Sex Signal: _____
Undercover Sex Signal: _____

7. Name the two signals that say, "I'm having a very good time with you!"
Undercover Sex Signal: _____
Undercover Sex Signal: _____

8. Name the three most suggestive signals that a woman might use when she is intoxicated, is very turned on, or is just exasperated that you didn't pick up on her first ones.
Undercover Sex Signal: _____
Undercover Sex Signal: _____
Undercover Sex Signal: _____

So, how did you think you did? Now, it's time to tally your score. Give yourself four points for every signal you answered correctly.

The Answers:

1. The 2 instinctive signals a woman who is attracted to you will do when you first walk into the room.

#20: The Perk-up (Breast Thrust)
She perks up, becomes more energetic and perhaps thrusts her breasts out

#25: The Pose
She strikes an attractive pose hoping you'll look her way

2. The 1 signal that two or more girls talking together will give if they like you:

#1: The Girlfriend Gab
If they like you, younger girls often will peek at you and giggle They might even cuddle with each other and point.

More sophisticated women will whisper in a more clan-destine fashion

3. Name 3 ways a woman across the room signals primarily with her eyes that she wants you:

#2: The Peek-a-Boo
She will peek at you over a book or menu

#3: The Shy Geisha
She will demurely look down and away. However, if she is interested in you, she will look up again in 45 seconds

#4: The Sidelong Glance
She will give you repeated sidelong glances even if she is conversing with someone else.

4. The 4 signals that involve a woman baring more skin to you to let you know you turn her on.

#6: The Exposé
She will pull her blouse or dress aside to entice you with more

#7: The Shoe Dangle
She will let one of her shoes dangle on her foot or toes, usually baring her sole

#14 The Underarm Flash
A woman who likes you will often take a pose like the old fashioned pin-up with one arm up and her hand behind her head—thus revealing her underarm. If you are chatting with her, she might raise her arm or rest it on a seat back to reveal her bare underarm.

#26: The Leg Show

Women have learned to use their legs enticingly in a number of ways to entice a man. She might pull her skirt up to reveal more leg or even separate them slightly to give you a quick peek.

5. The 4 signals involving distance that a woman sitting with you will throw to let you know she'd like more intimacy with you

#8: The Close Encounter

She will stand or sit closer to you than convention would ordinarily dictate. Sometimes she does this only fleetingly, but she expects you to pick up on it.

#9: The Space Invasion

A woman will either put an object or perhaps her arm or hand in your "personal zone" or "personal territory."

#10: The "Innocent" Touch

Nothing "innocent" about this one. If a woman touches your hand, your arm, or any other part of your body—however fleetingly—it means she is signaling you.

#11: The Lean-2-U

If it is not feasible to stand or sit too close to you, she might lean into your personal space. She also uses this tactic to show she is interested in what you are saying.

6. The 6 signals a woman gives with her hands that say, "You excite me."

#5: The Jewelry Tug

This often starts as an instinctive reaction because you make her nervous. More experienced women, however, realize that gently twisting a necklace or tugging an earring can be enticing to you because it calls attention to her cleavage or neck.

#12: The Weathervane Palm
A woman who does not like you or what you're saying might clench her fists while talking with you. If she's neutral, she might rest her head on her hands, knuckles forward. If, however, you turn her on, her hand will most likely turn around so that her palms are giving you a subtle "come hither" motion.

#13 The Necking
When foxes fight to the death, the loser bares her neck to the victor, taunting him to deliver the fatal piercing. When a woman pulls her hair aside, it is a subliminal (or contrived) sign of surrender.

#16 The Primp
A woman primping in front of you serves a duul purpose. She is not only making herself more attractive for you; she is drawing attention to herself

#17 The Hair Play
Women who are attracted to you will draw attention to their hair either by primping it, twisting it around their finger, or caressing it as though it were you doing so.

#18: The Self-Caress
A woman's "pleasure center" is distributed more equally throughout her body than yours so, when spotting a man she likes, it feels good to "pet" herself. Smart women, seeing men's positive reaction to her self-caresses, exaggerate them.

7. The 3 signals that say "I'm having a very good time with you!"

#19: The Shoulder Scrunch
This is the little girl coming out in her. The unspoken message is, "Ooh, I'm having a good time around you." If her shoulders are bare, she also knows you enjoy seeing her squiggle around.

#24: The Goofy Girl
Similarly, a little girl having fun will get goofy. The grown up version might have some sexual overtones like winking or putting something in her mouth, ear or nose.

#21: The Copy Cat
More sophisticated and knowledgeable women employ this neurolinguistic programming technique to show they are on the same "wave length" as you.

8. The 3 most suggestive signals that a woman might use when she is intoxicated, very turned on, or just exasperated that you didn't pick up on her first ones!

#15: The Lips Lick
These last three signals are quite suggestive. Licking her lips subliminally tells you, "You taste good to me."

#23 The Sexy Pet
The implications of rimming the bowl or stem of a glass with her finger, especially her middle finger needs little explanation.

#22: The Suggestive Suck
Ditto!

Did you get a 100 percent? "Wait a minute," I hear some of you guys with the more analytical, problem-solving type brains protesting. "If I got them all right, I'd have a score of 104 percent." You're right. But if you got them all correct, the only numbers you'd have to noodle over would be the notches on your headboard. Let me rephrase the question. Did you get all 26 correct? Hey, Romeo, congratulations! You'll never have any pick-up problems again.

Is your score a little closer to your hat size? Well, not to worry. All you need to do is go back a few pages and read the last 1000 words before The Quiz. Every signal is mentioned. Memorize them—and then start using them. You will be AMAZED at your success with women.

And then there will come a time in your life when *she* walks through the door. Many men know it the minute they lay eyes on her. Although scientists have declared, "love at first sight" is nothing more than a semantic term, they recognize its prevalence, especially with men.[75] In a Harvard study of men in love, it was found that they often knew they were goners by the fourth date (whereas many women weren't even sure they were in love by the 20th date.[76]) When this happens, you don't want to take any chances. You want to pull out all the artillery you've stockpiled from *Undercover Sex Signals* so far.

33

Diary of a Successful U.S.S. Man

I told my friend Phil the other day about *Undercover Sex Signals* and he asked me, "Are you writing it for scanners or seekers?" When I asked, "Huh?" he reminded me of something he'd told me a few years ago.

He said his relationship with women was like that with his car radio. When he was younger, he'd go racing down the highway of life, radio blaring full blast. He grooved on *scan*. "Oh, yeah," he said. "There'd be a few seconds of acid rock where I'd do that goofy head bop thing. Then—RRUCH—it would skip to rap music that I'd shout along with until—RRUCH—it became Country & Western. But, before they got to the end of the unrequited love story—RRUCH—I'd hear a few seconds of traffic and weather together. 'The temperature this afternoon will be'—RRUCH—strains of classical guitar interrupted before—RRUCH—Howard Stern came on shouting down some dumbass caller." Phil said this got confusing and tiring.

He scanned with women, too, trying to score with every one, and the same thing happened.

So he turned down the volume a bit, and found another sound track for his life. Now his radio was on *seek*. He'd seek for a while until he found a woman he liked. Then he'd stay until he tired of her. When he found himself wanting to drown out everything she said, he'd ram his thumb into the button and seek another.

At last, I think Phil has found the woman he can make beautiful music with forever, and I've never seen him happier. In our last conversation, he asked me please to pass on this wisdom to men. There's a time to scan, a time to seek, and a time to *set your button for keeps*.

For now, enjoy the scanning and seeking for all the women giving you undercover sex signals. With your newfound knowledge, you're a sexual polygraph machine and can be successful with every one of them. Just keep in mind that some day a "keeper" is going to walk through that door. And when she does, you will be ready for her.

So long for now, Stud-Muffin, er, I mean Dear Reader. Ashley, Jade, Sandy, Tanya, I, and millions of women around the world are heartened knowing that you are now a U.S.S. man. But please, don't forget to use this knowledge when we're giving you a U.S.S. across a crowded room! Remember that there's a time to scan, a time to seek, and a time to set your button for keeps.

For now, happy scanning!

References

1. Perper, Timothy. 1985. *Sex Signals: the Biology of Love*. Philadelphia: ISI Press
2. Sannito, Thomas, Ph.D., and Peter McGovern, J., J.D, Ed.D. 1985. *Courtroom Psychology for Trial Lawyers*. New York: John Wiley & Sons
3. *Time* magazine, Aug. 28, 2000, "Flying Solo"
4. Ibid.
5. Ibid.
6. Ibid.
7. Mead, Margaret. 1935. *Sex and Temperament in Three Primitive Societies*. New York: William Morrow
8. Malloy, T. E., A. Yarlas, R. K. Montvilo, and D. B. Sugarman. 1995. "Agreement and Accuracy in Children's Interpersonal Perceptions: a Social Relations Analysis." *Journal of Personality and Social Psychology*, 67, 692–702
9. Morman, Mark. T. and Kory Floyd. 1998 "Overt Expression of Affection in Male-Male Interaction." *Sex Roles: Journal of Research*, 38(9–10), 871.
10. Rabinowitz, F. E. 1991. "The Male-to-Male Embrace: Breaking the Touch Taboo in a Men's Therapy Group." *Journal of Counseling and Development*, 69, 574–576

11. Rubin, Zick. 1970. "Measurement of Romantic Love." *Journal of Personality and Social Psychology*, 16, 265–73

12. Ibid.

13. Walster, E., G. W. Walster, et al. 1973. "Playing Hard to Get; Understanding an Elusive Phenomenon." *Journal of Personality and Social Psychology*, 26:113–21

14. Peretti, Peter O., and Heidi Kippschull. 1989. "Influence of Five Types of Music on Social Behaviors of Mice." *Psychological Studies*, 35(2):98–103

15. Maslow, A. H. and N. L. Mintz. 1956. "Effects of Aesthetic Surroundings." *Journal of Psychology*, 41:247–254

16. Townsend, John M. and Gary D.Levy. 1990. "Effects of Potential Partners' Physical Attractiveness and Socioeconomic Status on Sexuality and Partner Selection." *Archives of Sexual Behavior*, 19(2):149–164

17. Aronson E., et al. 1966. "The Effect of a Pratfall on Increasing Interpersonal Attractiveness," *Psychonomic Science* 4:227–228

18. Kellerman, Joan, et al. 1989. "Looking and Loving: the Effects of Mutual Gaze on Feelings of Romantic Love." *Journal of Research in Personality*

19. Shotland, R., et al. 1988. "Can Men and Women Differentiate Between Friendly and Sexually Interested Behavior?" *Social Psychology Quarterly*, 51 (1), 66–73

20. Jones, Andrew John. 1982. "Nonverbal Flirtation Behavior: an Observational Study in Bar Settings." Unpublished masters thesis. New York State University at Plattsburgh

21. Moore, M. M. 1985. "Nonverbal Courtship Patterns in Women: Context and Consequences." *Ethnology and Sociobiology*, 6:237–247

22. Fisher, Helen. 1992. *Anatomy of Love*. New York: Fawcett Columbine.

23. McKeachie, W. J. 1952. "Lipstick as a Determiner of First Impressions of Personality." *Journal of Social Psychology*, 36, 241–244

24. Perper, Timothy. 1985. *Sex Signals: the Biology of Love*. Philadelphia: ISI Press
25. Sternberg, Robert J. 1988 *The Triangle of Love*, New York: Basic Books
26. Perper, Timothy. 1985. *Sex Signals: the Biology of Love*. Philadelphia: ISI Press
27. Bem, D. J. 1972. "Self Perception Theory." *Advances in Experimental Social Psychology*, 6:1–62
28. Perper, Timothy. 1985. *Sex Signals: the Biology of Love*. Philadelphia: ISI Press
29. *The Herald Tribune*, Feb. 24, 1999
30. Tennov, Dorothy. 1979. *Love and Limerance: the Experience of Being in Love*, New York: Stein and Day.
31. Bailey, Janet. 1989. "The Lure of the Rogue, Women's Obsessions for Men Who Are No Good." *Health*, 21 (12), 62–65
32. Graham, Dee, et al. 1995. "A Scale for Identifying Stockholm Syndrome Reactions in Young Dating Women." *Violence and Victims*, 10 (1): 3–22
33. Ibid.
34. Bailey, Janet. 1989. "The Lure of the Rogue, Women's Obsessions for Men Who Are No Good." *Health*, 21 (12), 62–65.
35. Graham, Dec, et al. 1995. "A Scale for Identifying Stockholm Syndrome Reactions in Young Dating Women." *Violence and Victims*, 10 (1); 3–22.
36. Kellerman, Joan, et al. 1989. "Looking and Loving: the Effects of Mutual Gaze on Feelings of Romantic Love." *Journal of Research in Personality*,
37. Fisher, Helen. 1992. *Anatomy of Love*. New York: Fawcett Columbine
38. Kellerman, Joan, et al. 1989. "Looking and Loving: The Effects of Mutual Gaze on Feelings of Romantic Love." *Journal of Research in Personality*,
39. Hasart, Julie K., and Kevin L. Hutchinson. 1997. "The Effects of

Eyeglasses on Perceptions of Interpersonal Attraction." *Journal of Social Behavior and Personality*, 8(3), 521–528

40. Money, John, Ph.D. 1986. *Lovemaps*. New York: Irvington Publishers

41. Ibid.

42. Lewis, Thomas, M.D., et al. 2000. *A General Theory of Love*. New York: Random House.

43. Byrne, D. 1971. *The Attraction Paradigm*. New York: Academic Press

44. Ibid.

45. Fisher, Helen. 1992. *Anatomy of Love*. New York: Fawcett Columbine

46. Cook, Mark and Robert McHenry, 1978. *Sexual Attraction*. New York: Pergamon Press

47. Perper, Timothy. 1985. *Sex Signals: the Biology of Love*. Philadelphia: ISI Press

48. Goleman, Daniel. 1989. "Brain's Design Emerges as a Key to Emotions," quoting Dr. Joseph LeDoux, psychologist at the Center for Neural Science at New York University. *New York Times*, Aug. 89

49. Oguchi, Takashi, et al. 1997 "Voice and Interpersonal Attraction." *Japanese Psychological Research*, 39 (1), 56–61

50. Cook, Mark. 1977. "Gaze and Mutual Gaze in Social Encounters." *American Scientist*, 65:328–333

51. Sternberg, Robert J. 1988. *The Triangle of Love*. Scranton, Pennsylvania. Basic Books

52. Perper, Timothy. 1985. *Sex Signals: the Biology of Love*. Philadelphia: ISI Press.

53. Arkowitz, H., et al. 1975 "The Behavioural Assessment of Social Competence in Males." *Behavioral Therapy*, 6, 3–13

54. Kerckhoff, C. and K. E. Davis, 1962. "Value Consensus and Need Complementarity in Mate Selection." *American Sociological Review*, 27:295–303

55. Fisher, Helen. 1992. *Anatomy of Love*. New York: Fawcett Columbine

56. Dutton, D. G. and A. P. Aron. 1974 "Some Evidence for Heightened Sexual Attraction Under Conditions of High Anxiety." *Journal of Personality and Social Psychology* 30:510–517

57. Maslow, A. H. and N. L. Mintz. 1956. "Effects of Aesthetic Surroundings." *Journal of Psychology* 41:247–254.

58. Izard, C. E. and M. C. Hyson. 1986. "Shyness as a Discreet Emotion" in Jones, W. H., J. M. Cheek, and S. R. Briggs (eds.), *Shyness: Perspectives on Research and Treatment* (pp. 147–160). New York: Plenum

59. "Shyness and Physical Attractiveness in Mixed-Sex Dyads." *Journal of Personality and Social Psychology*, 61, 35–49

60. Hamer, R. J. and M. A. Bruch. 1997. "Personality Factors and Inhibited Career Development: Testing the Unique Contribution of Shyness." *Journal of Vocational Behavior*, 50, 382–400

61. Bruch, M. A., S. Giordano, and L. Pearl. 1986. "Differences Between Fearful and Self-conscious Shy Subtypes in Background and Current Adjustment." *Journal of Research in Personality*, 20, 172–186

62. Sanderson, W. C., P. A. DiNardo, R. M. Rapee, and D. H. Barlow. 1990. "Syndrome Co-morbidity in Patients Diagnosed with a DSM-III-Revised Anxiety Disorder." *Journal of Abnormal Psychology*, 99, 308–312

63. Capsi, A., G. H. Elder and D. J. Bern. 1988. "Moving Away From the World: Life-course Patterns of Shy Children." *Developmental Psychology*, 24, 824–831

64. Bruch, M. A., J. M. Gorsky, T. M. Collins and P. A. Berger. 1989. "Shyness and Sociability Reexamined: A Multicomponent Analysis." *Journal of Personality and Social Psychology*, 57, 904–915

65. Cheek, J. M. and A. H. Buss. 1981. "Shyness and Sociability." *Journal of Personality and Social Psychology*, 41, 330–339.

66. *New York Times*, Oct. 20, 1998

67. Cook, Mark, and Robert McHenry. 1978. *Sexual Attraction.* New York: Pergamon Press

68. Ibid.

69. *New York Times,* Jan. 18, 2001. Quoting Dr. Joseph Walther, an associate professor of communication, social psychology and information technology at Rensselaer Polytechnic Institute

70. Walster, Elaine, William G. Walster, and Ellen Berscheid. 1978. *Equity: Theory and Research.* Boston: Allyn and Bacon

71. Mathews, A. M., et al. 1972. "The Principal Components of Sexual Preference." *British Journal of Social Clinical Psychology* 11:35–43

72. Butler, Jeff, et al. 1998. "Impression Formation as a Function of Male Baldness." *Perceptual and Motor Skills,* 86(1), 347–354

73. Mathews, A. M., et al. 1972 "The Principal Components of Sexual Preference." *British Journal of Social Clinical Psychology,* 11,35–43

74. Townsend, John M., and Gary D. Levy. 1990. "Effects of Potential Partners' Physical Attractiveness and Socioeconomic Status on Sexuality and Partner Selection." *Archives of Sexual Behavior,* 19(2), 149–164.

75. Murstein, Bernard I., Ph.D. 1980. "Love at First Sight: a Myth." *Medical Aspects of Human Sexuality,* 14(9)

76. Kanin, E. J., K. D. Davidson and S. R. Scheck. 1970. "A Research Note on Male-Female Differentials in the Experience of Heterosexual Love." *The Journal of Sex Research,* 6: 64–72